THE JOYFUL WARRIOR

How to be Free in an Unfree world.
Entrepreneurial Activism for first time founders.

THE JOYFUL WARRIOR

How to be Free in an Unfree world.
Entrepreneurial Activism for first time founders.

Gemma Roe

Published by Go Rogue UK

www.go-rogue.co.uk

For Dawn

5 June 1961 – 11 February 2022

TABLE OF CONTENTS

ACKNOWLEDGEMENTS

There is an old African proverb that reads, 'If you want to go fast, go alone; but if you want to go far, go together.' This saying especially resonates with the creation of this book. It has taken many years to collate, collaborate, and gather incredible insights to ensure the value of this work. This book, the first in a trilogy, is dedicated to the late Dawn Gibbins MBE, whose influence played a pivotal role in my journey into entrepreneurship.

I extend my heartfelt thanks to my coach, Nick Williams, who provided me with the courage and stamina to explore new horizons and believe in myself. I am immensely grateful to those who contributed to the book, including Sahar Hashemi OBE, Nicola Huelin, Tom Hodgkinson and Hanna Sillitoe; your contributions mean the world to me. Of course, this book wouldn't be here if it weren't for the incredible work of two very sensible and insightful editors. Alex Johnson guided me during the initial two years, and then the baton was passed to Peter Howe, who helped shape and structure the final manuscript, smoothing out the rough edges.

My journey into writing might never have begun without my AltMBA tribe, particularly Laura Hall and Fredrik Rahka. Seth Godin has shown me that a Joyful Warrior never stops creating.

I offer my heartfelt gratitude to all my former and current business partners, industry associates, and employees. You've taught me that the path of a warrior is never a straight line and that no (wo)man is an island. Our most profound lessons, failures, and successes can be found in the nature and quality of our relationships. I also want to thank my incredible friends who proofread early drafts, including Lucy, my inspiring sister, and to my soulful, thoughtful clients – Jane, Emma, Michelle, Naomi, Juliet, and friends in the industry who have kept me buoyant and cheered me on. There are so many of you, and my appreciation list in this regard is endless.

Lastly, I might never have found the courage to complete this book without the love of my beautiful children, Esmee and Eli. Despite being neglected for a significant part of their weekends and school holidays while I locked myself away to write, they have been my greatest source of inspiration. They continue to inspire me to work harder than ever, securing a better world for their future.

FOREWORD

Nicola Huelin
Award-winning Business Coach and Mentor

In the summer of 2002, age 29, I sat on my usual, crowded commuter train, staring at a small piece of gold ribbon in the palm of my hand. In that moment, for the first time in my career, I realised my life would never be the same.

At the time, I was a business consultant, selected to join a small group to take part in a six-month programme designed to fast track high-potentials to executive level. On the very first day, the trainer shared a story which changed my life in ways I couldn't begin to imagine. He pulled out a long piece of golden ribbon from his pocket. Holding it out at arm's length the other end almost touched the floor.

'Imagine this piece of ribbon represents your life,' he said, scanning the room, surveying our group of twelve corporate rising stars. 'Does anyone know what the average life expectancy is?' We all looked at each other, bounced a few numbers around and ultimately agreed that it was probably about 83. 'Good,' said the trainer, as he took a large pair of orange-handled scissors from his trouser pocket. 'Now what's the average age of everyone in this room today?' I was by far the youngest at 29, but we settled on 40. The trainer immediately opened the blades of his big steel scissors and slashed half to the floor. The room fell silent. I'm not sure which felt more depressing to the group – seeing the half of our lives laying spent on the ground or noticing how much shorter the remaining piece had suddenly become. 'On average, how much time do we spend sleeping?' he continued. It turned out I wasn't the only one who needs eight hours minimum sleep a night in order not to become dysfunctional. The scissors struck again. Another third gone.

'Drinking and eating?' he asked next. It's important to add, our group embodied the 'eat-on-the-go, grab-what-you-can' and 'consider-yourself-lucky-to-have-eaten-at-all' kind of culture. He chopped another five percent for 'survival eating'. Next up... 'Travelling?' Not holidays or family visits, just essential, routine travel – getting from A to B. We all commuted to our work, anything up to 90 minutes each way. Another chunk of ribbon fell to the ground. All eyes were on the trainer's startlingly stubby remaining piece of ribbon, which barely stretched from wrist to fingertips.

'This,' he said, 'is the part of your life you have left to live. The remainder of your life that you have any control over what you do with. If, and only if, you're lucky enough to live to the ripe old age of 83!'

BOSH! It hit me like a ton of bricks! The whole group seemed to have been hit. That remaining stub still included the time spent at work and we spent a LOT of our time working. But it didn't stop there for me. That day, I was the only woman in the room. Nobody had begun to factor in all the other things that snipped away at my ribbon – the lion's share of the washing, cooking, ironing, cleaning, shopping, tidying, after-school activities – all the things we do to make a home and raise a family.

As a mother, the million dollar question emblazoned across my mind was, 'How on earth am I going to find time to spend quality time with my daughter?' My daughter was 5, so I figured I had thirteen years of 'at home' motherhood left before she most likely headed off to higher education when she turned 18 (little did I know at the time, this would be an overestimation, as my daughter left home at 16 to pursue her passions at a performing arts school in another part of the country). I had already started feeling like I was living for the weekends and as I became more successful in my career, I became increasingly 'money-rich and time-poor'. From the outside looking in I was successful, especially for my age, but in that Golden Ribbon Moment I suddenly knew: if I was going to continue feeling as 'successful' on the inside as I appeared to the outside world ... I needed to do something different.

Perhaps you've already had a golden ribbon moment in your life? A moment where something happens (redundancy, a new baby, illness, loss, a new opportunity) or something is said to you (in a book, a friend, family, colleague, article or perhaps a whisper from your heart and soul) that makes you realise it's time for a change. Maybe you're still working full-time in your day job? Maybe you've already left the corporate world and feel ready for something new? Or perhaps you're thinking of starting up a business as a side hustle? Wherever you are right now, it's never too late – or too soon – to start creating the life, freedom and impact that's important to you. Perhaps reading this book is your next step towards claiming your purpose, making a change in your career and tapping into your inner warrior to find the inspiration and courage you need to move forward.

Soon after my golden ribbon moment, I walked away from my corporate career. Friends and family thought I was crazy – some even told me so. The internet was in its infancy, social media hadn't been born. I thought I was the only crazy one taking this 'terriciting' (my word for half terrifying, half exciting) leap of faith. I'd have to wait a few more years, for technology to evolve and social media to open up my world of crazy entrepreneurship to realise I was FAR from alone.

Women all around the world were answering their own callings to embark on their own pioneering journeys into the world of entrepreneurship. Never have the opportunities been more abundant. Never has the need for our contributions been greater. Today there are millions of us. Each making our difference, as we take our vision of what success means to us, and the difference we feel called to make, and turn it into a reality.

If my twenty years of being an entrepreneur have taught me anything, it's that success is never a straight-line journey, and it doesn't always feel easy. If it was, we'd all be doing it and there would be nobody left to (wo)man the corporate ships. But for those who hear the call (and as you've picked up this book, this likely includes you) there is a parallel world waiting to be discovered by pioneers ready to blaze their own trail.

Hindsight is a wonderful thing. There's no way I could have predicted the incredible business and lifestyle I'm blessed to enjoy today. One thing is certain though, I would never be where I am today, if I didn't begin. Would I take the same leap of faith, if I could rewind time? A million times over! The path is paved with opportunities where building and growing your own business that's a force for good in the world, is one of the most rewarding, fulfilling and inspiring adventures of a lifetime. A source of ultimate joy! It is also one of the most powerful paths for learning and personal growth, that at times requires the spirit, determination and commitment of a warrior. A warrior who leads from the heart. If any of this resonates with you, you're in the right place.

You hold in your hands a treasure chest of insights, inspiration and wisdom from Gemma and the other successful entrepreneurs she brings together. I can't imagine a better guide to introduce you to this new world. A pioneer in sustainable and ethical business herself, Gemma has already made such a positive impact in our world. She's been there, done it and got the T-shirts. She has experienced the good, the bad and the ugly. What's more she is on a mission to help others just like you. If you're reading to embrace the ultimate business adventure that brings joy, while equipped with the wisdom and strength of a warrior, read on.

Welcome to the world of The Joyful Warrior.

Nicola Huelin

P.S. I have an invitation for you. Once you've read what follows in these pages, come back to this page and answer these questions:

What would you do if you knew you couldn't fail? Knowing what you know now, what will you do next? When will you begin?

THE DEN

The best way to predict your future is to create it.

Abraham Lincoln

'Sorry, but I'm not convinced.'

With the exception of a squeak from the wheels of camera equipment and the gentle swoosh of a boom mic passing over our heads, it was excruciatingly silent. Duncan Bannatyne dropped his pen heavily onto the notebook beside him before making his final declaration. 'I'm out.'

It was then that I could feel the red hot tingling burn of humiliation. Suddenly, the realisation hit me.

I'd made the biggest mistake of my life.

As I stood there, being interrogated on a national television show, scheduled to be broadcast to 2.1 million viewers. I started to feel like a total fool. Sweating profusely under a hot spotlight, on a dark stage, melting my career down to a greasy pool of nothingness in the most public and desperate of situations. How had I not realised that it could go so wrong? I would never have signed up for this had I known how ridiculous I would look. Hadn't I understood that public humiliation was a very real risk? The incessant internal criticism raced through my mind as the hope and anticipation slowly left my body. It was draining down through my legs and out though the studio floor. This was replaced with a cold and paralysing fear which crept into my skin and wrapped around my body until it had consumed me entirely. My business partner and I shifted uneasily from foot to foot and cast our terrified gaze to the last and final Dragon...

Theo Paphitis was scribbling in his notebook. A dappled shaft of sunlight peeked through the darkened studio window behind him. He lifted his pen from the paper, paused for one moment as he contemplated his move, and then turned his gaze towards us.

He smiled. Then shifted in his seat, ready to address us. The energy was different this time. I felt a small flutter of hope resurface. 'I'm going to make you an offer,' he said. 'But,' he paused, 'not on the terms you've asked for...'

After a lengthy to-and-fro negotiation between my business partner Aidan Quinn and Theo Paphitis we staggered out of the Den with feelings of disbelief, excitement and amazement. We'd received an offer of £75,000 for 40% of the business, O-Pod Buildings (a small manufacturing firm which produced small, steel-framed circular garden offices). This included a hilariously complicated 50% buy-back scheme suggested by Aidan as a way to reduce the equity we'd have to release long term. It was an entertaining exchange, but I couldn't help but feel it could leave us in a worse position in the long run.

Over the coming months it became clear that this new business relationship wasn't to be. Aidan was struggling with the idea of losing so much of his company. He was the founder and designer behind O-Pod and he'd invested a huge amount of his personal savings and energy into the project. Aidan's infectious humour and devil-may-care attitude were his greatest attributes. As an entrepreneur and free-thinker he had a clear disdain for bureaucracy and preferred to do things his own way. Taking business instruction from a stranger in a suit was always going to be difficult for him. We had many discussions about what we should do. On top of which, I discovered that I was pregnant with my first child. The odds seemed against us. We made a difficult decision and walked away from the deal. And I walked away from O-Pod.

That was over a decade ago. Since that white-knuckle ride on Dragons' Den, I've climbed, scrambled, crawled and dragged my way through the tumultuous early days of the life of a start-up entrepreneur. The path has been interwoven with unimaginable challenges and utterly inconceivable highs. Like any adrenaline sport, I found that the secret to remaining in the game as a start-up entrepreneur is largely down to two things. A blatant disregard for safety and a steadfast desire to reach faraway horizons and summits which would terrify most people.

I began my first enterprise as a single mum on income support, from the kitchen table, with no experience and no capital. Building my website at night and bootstrapping the start-up costs from my meagre child allowance. I know one thing for sure. If I did it, in the most difficult of circumstances, so, my friend, can you.

Along the journey, you'll discover the dizzying peaks of euphoria swiftly followed by rapidly descending slopes of despair. The dip is what some silicon valley entrepreneurs call 'the struggle'. The struggle presents itself multiple times throughout your journey, so prepare for it! My established and successful start-up, finally hitting the £1million revenue mark was the most valuable learning experience of my entire career.

Ultimately, success in the business brought with it a whole host of problems including the toxic collusion of corporate misconduct, fraud and shareholder scandal on a scale I could never have anticipated in my wildest dreams. I knew years prior to my exit that it was time to go. Clinging on to a defective albeit successful business model, entangled with people who didn't share the same sense of ethics and values will simply never work for a start-up founder. My work as a founder was complete. Founding a business, my dear reader, is the attainment of true freedom and joy. What you do with your business once you've scaled it is entirely up to you.

But, I believe that you have the capacity to build something beautiful. Once you've done it several times, you can then teach others, or continue on as Richard Branson and develop hundreds of businesses. Who knows? But, you must start something. The world needs you.

Although this book is written primarily for women, it's not a book about feminism. Neither is it exclusively about the nuances of business start-ups.

This is a book about a great civilisation, a burgeoning eight billion human beings, all coexisting on an immense spinning ball, coalescing at a definite crossroads in their evolution. This is a book about those who have shaped the world before us, and those who are yet to come. This book is about the woman who lies awake at night worrying about single-use plastics and the plight of the albatross. Those who look at their children and wonder what they might face in their lifetimes. This is a book about the sperm whale, the food chain, the factory, the retailer and the magnificent species who are seemingly hurtling along this trajectory with us.

This is a book about you.

For nothing can change while we all remain the same. Yet, no single person feels it possible that they can have any effect whatsoever. But what if we weren't in this alone? What could each of us do to benefit us personally, locally and nationally? For one thing unites us all; and one thing alone can be held responsible for, and capable of, real change. From the ground up. And that's business.

I can imagine you now, wrinkling your nose at the mere suggestion of 'business' when there's talk of radical change for the benefit of the sperm whale and the albatross. What image conjures into your mind when you hear the word 'business'? Have you evoked the caricature of the middle-aged man in a grey suit, holding a briefcase, possibly driving a sports car? I hear you. I used to think this, too.

But now when I think of business, I think of freedom. Creativity. Of joy. Prosperity. Leadership and empowerment. Most importantly, incredible, refreshing and revitalising change. Like the gathering momentum of a fresh, cool breeze rippling though a bleached and heat-parched valley. A distant rumble of thunder as the breeze buffets the dry grasses, the tangible energy of impending rain, envisaged as a collection of rolling, bruised storm clouds gathering on the horizon. This is the power I sense gathering in the psyche of the awakening female. So, stick with me, because you and I together are going to explore the 'old world' of entrepreneurship and the 'new world' which awaits us all. So jump on in, and let's dust ourselves down and kick that grey-suited man and his ridiculous sports car into the past where he rightfully belongs.

HOW TO BE FREE IN AN UNFREE WORLD

There is no power on earth apart from business capable of making the changes we desperately need for the continued survival of the planet.

Anita Roddick

I believe that inside each and every one of us is the creative spark of an entrepreneur. The mere fact that you've selected this book amidst the plethora of others is an indicator that you can hear the call, albeit merely a whisper. The book you hold in your hands is my rallying cry to you. A call to arms. A war cry. Because we need you. This is a book, above all else, which is reaching out to speak directly to you.

Urging you to bring forth your ideas and join me in the creation game. Why?

Because I believe that the world has been shaped unrecognisably by industry. Furthermore, I believe that industry can shape it back again. Considerately. Carefully. Kindly.

I have learnt both through my research and through personal experience that being successful is not simply down to luck or money. It's more often down to the mindset which successful business owners cultivate through discipline, faith and vision. It's learned behaviour. It's a mindset which you, too, can cultivate.

The stories, research and interviews in this book will carry you a little way into the philosophy of active entrepreneurship. It's my sincere hope that the encouragement found within these pages will assist you with unearthing your creativity and may enable you to step forwards to take your rightful place amongst other female entrepreneurs who are working tirelessly to forge a new earth through the vehicle of their businesses. I can teach you what differentiates a successful entrepreneur from a self-employed person who's stuck in a rut. I'll light the way for you. See me as your lighthouse. I'll cast a wide beam of light across the stormy, dark and turbulent sea of uncertainty. This is the knowledge I wish someone had shared with me before I'd started out. You are soon to embark on a distilled decade of drama, sleepless nights, dark alleys, wrong turns, surprising successes and much painfully accumulated knowledge.

So, I'm sharing a story with you. Both my story and stories and experiences of others which will help you on your way. The sharing of stories is how we communicate ideas and knowledge. Since our great ancestors sat around fires and told tales of foreign lands, we've always transferred knowledge this way. At the time of writing this, in 2023, we are at a tangible crossroads as a global society; I am sharing knowledge with you in the hope that you can locate the entrepreneur within yourself and find the courage to launch your idea. Your idea matters more than you could ever know. Your idea could be something which really does impact other people in a way which we might never imagine. Your idea could inspire others to also embark on their journey. It's my hope that your idea could very well be a solution to one of the myriad of problems which we all face. This, is how we'll save the world.

Within the pages of this book, you will have direct access to both my experiences and those of other entrepreneurs. Brave souls who have built their businesses from scratch. Underpinning the guidance in this book is a dramatic personal story of hope, fear, courage and crushing disappointment. I feel it important that I share with you the lessons gleaned from my company, which was at one point a real success, before being beset by tragedy and disaster. Tragedy and failure through action as a start-up entrepreneur are the most incredible learning opportunities. The precious lessons learnt, I know, you could most certainly benefit from. This is a book about a start-up. Your start-up, to be precise. It's imperative that you join myself and the millions of others out there striving to create a better world through our businesses. See me as your guide. Let me point out the dangers before you dive in. I can lead you up the mountain but you must walk the path with me. Get those walking books laced up my friend and ready for action, because, you and I – we're off on an adventure.

Given the crisis we've recently seen unfold before us over the past few years, and the emerging evolution of our global economy, your dreams may seem even more unattainable than ever. But, I assure you, the opportunity for you is immense. Not despite pandemics, wars and economic uncertainties but because of them. The world needs problem solvers, and entrepreneurs are, in their very nature, problem solvers.

Often feeling small, like a little cog in a gigantic wheel, we each pedal furiously within the machine. Striving to create a better life for ourselves. We convince ourselves that we are free and we busy ourselves with myriad activities, hobbies, friends and work. But still, many of us feel anxious. One thing after another stacking up in our armoury of potential threats.

But how about we reframe this in our own minds to benefit ourselves rather than restrict our aspirations? You see, it's my belief that with change comes great opportunity. Each shift that occurs in the geopolitical climate, a crevasse splits open in the bedrock of our society, rippling out across industry, fuelled by consumer demand. Those who are quick to produce ideas and solutions to solve problems or obstacles arising from current day events will undoubtedly forge success for themselves and their employees. These shifts in our social and economic systems present fantastic opportunities for entrepreneurs. Take, for example, a chemical cleaning company based in the North of England. The husband and wife team spent decades building their dry cleaning and cleaning products business. Unfortunately for them, they'd hit hard times and were almost at the point of financial ruin in 2019. Moments before closing their doors to the world and losing their home, the pandemic hit. As a remarkable twist of fate, they happened to have one product in their inventory which was suddenly in national demand. Hand Sanitiser! Tens of thousands of litres of the stuff! Not only did their product value shoot up instantaneously, but huge orders flooded in from corporate bodies such as the NHS and other commercial businesses across the entire country. This remarkable crisis actually saved their business, paid off their mortgage and ensured financial security for many years to come. A problem for many became an opportunity for those who were supplying the right product, at the right time.

Not all opportunities arise so suddenly. Some trends are identifiable years ahead of the opportunity. Consider for a moment, the popularity of plant-based foods in the western world. I believe this to be driven largely by the aspirations of the Millennial generation. This is now a long-term, sustainable and lucrative market which might not have arisen without social media. An upsurge of one market (smartphones) thereby creates an opportunity for another (plant-based food). As social media appeared rapidly onto the screens of every young person with a smartphone, so too did their knowledge of global and environmental issues.

Never before has one generation had the power to affect industry on such an enormous scale. This is a whole evolutionary shift of consumer spending and with the ethical consumer now seeking a different way to shop, there seems to be little slowing down. With each generation, markets must keep up with the aspirations of the consumer. For it is their spending power which fuels your business. There are still so many markets which are lagging behind when it comes to matching the speed of the Knowledge Revolution. The exponential *speed of knowledge* – and the upswing of new trends in travel, food, transport and lifestyle, means there is an exponential *increase in opportunity* for you, my dear, soon-to-be founder.

But, OK, let's play devil's advocate for a second. You identify an opportunity. How on earth can one person with no start-up capital actually get a foothold? Don't you need an inheritance or an investor to build a business? Not always. Not if you are brave enough to take the bootstrapped route. You can do this, without investment, but you must be able to set aside the time and determination to make it work. It's a common misconception that entrepreneurs are only those who've inherited large fortunes or are simply born lucky. I can honestly tell you that I embarked upon my career as a single mum, in a two-bedroomed cottage in England, living off food vouchers and with no capital whatsoever.

But, generating a great idea comes first from understanding yourself. Knowing your own mind so well that you create something which aligns with your vision for your future. Creating something for yourself which is so critical to your happiness must come from a place of true authenticity. Being an entrepreneur quite simply means to create something which didn't exist before. A new product, a service, or if you're really lucky, an entire industry. Once it's out in the world and generating a lifestyle for you, you'll be stuck with it for some time to come. Before I launch into the platitudes which you've heard too many times – 'Follow your passion ...

Do what makes you happy...' – I'll spin my own perspective on why these phrases are so persistent.

Simply put, in order to really create something truly magnificent, and truly you, it must align so closely with your core self that it radiates out of you like a sunbeam.

From what I've learnt over the past decade of my own start-up, and researching the journey of a multitude of others, there is one factor which truly unites the successful entrepreneurs. This special success factor is at the heart of this book, and yes, you guessed it. Purpose. You and your purpose. Your raison d'etre. The real, unashamedly authentic, shining and determined you. I found my purpose by sheer chance, and it's continually evolving as I align more with it. When you find your purpose, you will be unstoppable. This is why I felt it imperative to share with you some key start-up lessons, words of motivation and ridiculously important warnings, to enable you to discover and align with yours.

Moreover, you may find more than one purpose. For example, with my business activities, my purpose is to connect people to nature, through the design of eco-buildings and championing the remarkable skills of ethical builders. But my purpose, at this very moment, is to help you unearth what it is that's driving you. The authentic side of you that has been with you for your whole life. The restless spirit which whispers to your subconscious urging you to abandon your current reality and take the leap. We will be on a journey to unearth it. This book will assist you with finding the courage to accept where you are, decide where you want to be, and take the first steps to get there. Once you find your key purpose, you will notice others which feed into it. From there, the world, my friend, is yours.

Making the declaration to take the rest of your working life into your own hands through the vehicle of your career is probably the most important step you will ever take in your life. By starting out as an entrepreneur, you could very easily reach a point where you discover that you never have to work again. Equally, you could create a career for yourself that doesn't feel like work at all, simply how you choose to live and express yourself. Total freedom. Now if that's not worth a try, I don't know what is.

THE WAKE-UP CALL

Man cannot discover new oceans unless
he has the courage to lose sight of the shore.

André Gide

winner Nobel Prize in Literature

I had never planned to become an entrepreneur. In fact, it was never a profession that was highlighted or even suggested by careers advice at school. Nor did my parents recognise it as a viable prospect for my future. It's as if it's a secret profession, a hidden world, kept off the table as many adolescents consider subjects for their A levels or university courses.

Of course, there have always been business and accounting university degrees available. Many of these graduates can run corporate organisations and find their way around a balance sheet. However, the type of entrepreneur I'm talking about here isn't taught in a traditional sense. They are discovered. Ordinary people who have discovered this latent creativity, usually accidentally, like a precious jewel hidden under layers of sediment for millennia, that is one day dug up as a dull pebble, dusted off, cut, faceted, cleaned and polished. In its new glistening state it shines for all to see and it's difficult to imagine that it was once an ordinary stone that didn't freely share its light.

I think daily life and the impact of those around us can push us in either direction. Either bury us deeper into the immovable earth or free us and polish away our ingrained beliefs and restrictions to reveal our more creative and authentic powerful selves. Without the right support, life can swallow us up in quicksand so we slowly become part of the hard, parched earth. It takes a monumental effort to dispel the hardened beliefs that are built up over decades of conditioning and find the shining jewel inside us. But it just takes a spark to set us on the road, a kind word of encouragement from a friend or relative, a call to action from a book or a television programme, or an opportunity given to you by your boss or another entrepreneur who brings you into their world.

From the age of 7, up until about 10 years old, I was a die-hard eco-warrior. As the middle child of five children growing up on a farm in West Berkshire, I would try, in vain, to bring my siblings and parents around to my way of thinking. My bedroom walls were plastered with Save The Rainforest stickers and posters of whales and elephants. I'd spend hours painstakingly painting cardboard recycling boxes for my parents and sticking my Save The Planet stickers all over the house. I'd be collecting injured hedgehogs off the side of the road and digging newts out of the pond to keep and observe in a plastic goldfish bowl beside my bed. I could watch those newts for hours. It was a trait that my family endured. My passion for protecting the natural world was so strong that I joined numerous charities such as Greenpeace and the World Wildlife Fund. I donated what I could of my pocket money and read the newsletters which came through, in earnest.

The straw that finally broke the camel's back was a phone call my mother received one day from Greenpeace. I'd signed up to join an anti-whaling mission off the south coast of England and the ship set sail in seven days. They'd called to make travel arrangements and check I was suitably prepared.

'She's not coming,' my mother growled down the phone.

'Oh, sorry, may I ask why?'

'Because she's TEN!'

With that, the phone crashed back into the cradle with such force that the house shook to its rafters and that was the unfortunate end to the start of my environmental activism days.

By the time I'd reached my early twenties I'd inexplicably found a place in the world of mortgage finance and secured lending. Dressed in a pinstripe suit and clicking around in my high heels, I'd reached adulthood and proudly held a respectable job. Working up from an administrative position to the role of a senior underwriter and team leader was pleasing my young and ardent ego. I was sent on numerous management and sales courses and was gradually building up a satisfactory career for myself. Hitting £multimillion monthly targets for my employer meant that I was earning a pretty decent salary for someone of my age. My colleagues and I worked hard and were rewarded with days at the horse races and glitzy evening events with free bars at expensive hotels courtesy of the finance broker we worked for. My boss, a man called Rupert, smoked cigars and had chauffeurs. His hundreds of employees, of which I was one, were of course, in awe of him. My life was set on a trajectory in the corporate world and I was blissfully happy. My parents were delighted with my career choice and I didn't think that life could get much better. Time revolved around either the office, gym or my social life and I didn't think too deeply about anything other than my immediate needs. Coming into work every day to a full and vibrant office block among several hundred other young and hungry individuals was motivating and exciting. I felt secure. I was working hard from 8.30 a.m. until 7 p.m. most days until the weekend hit when I'd most likely be in a nightclub or bar spending my hard-earned cash slamming shots of tequila and Jägermeister so that I'd rarely remember getting home. This was normal, this was what I perceived as a successful career. And I loved it.

At the age of 25, my boyfriend and I decided to take an around the world trip. It was a three-year career break for us and we couldn't wait to hit the beaches and live from a backpack. We planned to travel overland through South East

Asia, to Malaysia and Indonesia and then on to Australia and New Zealand, where we would live for two years on a working permit.

As we were arranging the trip, a friend gave me the book, *Go it Alone* by Geoff Burch. If you have time, I suggest you seek this book out and read it immediately. The cover had an illustration of a man in a pinstripe suit, straining to take a step forward but hampered by a ball and chain. It was an introduction to self-employment and highlighted the fact that we are all at the mercy of our employers. It was this book which first opened the gateway in my mind to the possibility that perhaps I, too, could one day be self-employed. Doing exactly what, I had no idea. It was an alien reality to me, for people who had a strange and exotic talent I couldn't even imagine possessing. I toyed with the idea of a market stall or a smoothie bar. But really, I didn't have the foggiest. Besides, I was happy enough working my way up in my career. My employer was putting me on management training courses. There was progression. The money was good.

The finance industry was booming. My family thought it was madness to go abroad at this point in my career, gravely warning me that a gap in my CV would look unfavourable to future employers. Please, I urge you, if you have the opportunity to create a gap in your CV, do it without hesitation. You might just discover something which could set you off on another, more lucrative or fulfilling path.

It was after ten months travelling in South East Asia that something pressed my recalibration button. Spending so much time out of my usual routine, away from the buzz of the office and away from my life in the corporate world, really focused my mind. Without seeing a television for almost a year and remaining far away from western culture and contemporary life, I slowly and involuntarily awoke from my slumber.

In rural Cambodia, our tuk-tuk driver Simon, eager to show us his other line of work, drove us across some open farmland to a small grove of tall, swaying sugar palm trees. Barefoot, he sprung upon the nearest, wrapped his feet around the trunk and in a series of agile jumps, climbed up it in a matter of seconds. At the top of the tree, swaying perilously 30 ft above us, he swung his machete out from his waistband, cut the fruit from the upper branches, and just as quickly as he'd climbed up, he deftly made his way back down. The whole process took just a couple of minutes until he was proudly handing the freshly harvested fruit to us, the astonished open-mouthed tourists. As we stood under the scorching sun, he asked us what we did for a living. David explained that we worked in finance, selling mortgages for banks. Simon didn't understand. So, David broke it down to articulate that we sat in an office every day and worked on computers and telephones, effectively 'selling money' to people who needed loans. Simon was perplexed. I doubt that he had ever seen a call centre, certainly not the scale of the one we had in city centre Manchester. It was clear to me that the concept hadn't yet reached his village. I prayed that it never would.

Then we flew to Borneo.

I had always thought Borneo was a jungle, an island of primary rainforest. The image I had in my mind was something along the lines of 'Tomb Raider', with ancient relics and temple ruins strewn throughout the jungle, filled with the sound of hornbills and toucans and swinging, chattering monkeys.

As the small propeller plane descended through the cloud, my face was squashed up against the window, waiting for my first glimpse of the jungle canopy... But it didn't look like Borneo. The scorched orange earth lay out beneath me like a soiled patchwork quilt, scarred and scratched, interspersed with palm oil plantations and loggers' roads. I couldn't see the forest.

It had gone.

The 8-year-old eco-warrior who had been hidden away, concealed deep inside me for almost two decades, woke up from somewhere I hadn't realised existed. I didn't know what I felt most. Rage? Sorrow? Helplessness? I certainly felt cheated that the reality was not matching up with the 'Raiders of the Lost Ark' plane journey I had imagined. I sobbed for all of these equally important and confusing reasons as the plane made its bumpy descent. I cried pretty much every day for a week after that.

I am happy to report that I have never been the same again. That was STEP 1 towards finding my purpose. I had woken up.

FINDING YOUR PURPOSE

All children are born geniuses. 999 out of every 1,000 are swiftly and inadvertently degeniused by adults.

Buckminster Fuller

If your ultimate mission and primary interest in life lies hidden deep inside you, it may have already presented itself to you, in the same way that the Borneo experience did with me.

Have you had an experience where you watched something with disbelief and felt dismay that this is reality? Is there something which has shocked you about our society or are you worried about an issue which isn't being addressed or managed properly? Have any products disappointed you recently or made you question the design style or function?

What were you interested in when you were a child and how did you like to play? More importantly, what problems have you faced and how might you overcome them? Is there a product you need which isn't available to you? Where have you hoped for change but failed to find anyone doing anything about it?

Your emotions can be a powerful tool and a good indication of where your energy and interest lies. If you can fuel yourself through recognising your emotional state you can then use this to motivate yourself to act effectively. Recognising when you feel uplifted or enthusiastic and what it's connected to is an excellent way to understand where you could expand into this and design a great project. Feeling aggravated about something could also indicate that change is needed, and you may just be the person to do something about it.

You may feel inclined to bury deep feelings and pretend that it's someone else's problem. You have a life to live, work to do, children to feed and you're doing OK, thank you very much. Besides, aren't there other people out there doing this kind of thing? Charities, governments, volunteers? Well, perhaps there are. But have you stopped to consider that a problem or issue that isn't being effectively managed has presented itself to you for a reason and it may be within your reach *to do something about it*? We were all born with the capacity to do something impactful with our lives. Is this the sign you need that your path is *in that direction*? Could you alter the trajectory of your life so that you can: (a) discover who you really are and what you're capable of, (b) be a part of something and contribute towards solving a problem, and

(c) advance your professional life, access more resources/ wealth, and boost your sense of self-worth at the same time?

If you have had an experience which generated a strong emotional response, it's critical that you recognise how it made you feel and pay attention to what you would like to see done about it. You are seeing these problems for a reason. They are yours. Own them. Think about them. Only you have the perspective of the person who has experienced this problem first hand. Elon Musk is not going to dive in and fix this for you. He's preoccupied with his rockets. *You* have noticed something which is affecting your life directly (or at least, is triggering your emotional state), so *you* are the best placed person to act on it with the objectivity of real life experience.

I was distraught at seeing the absence of trees in Borneo. What does this say about me? That I care deeply about forests and jungles. That I love trees and the natural world. Strangely enough, anyone in my family could have told me about this as a small child but I don't think I had remembered or recognised this in my adult life. It just didn't correlate with the life I was living. That wasn't the 'me' who was working in finance, living in a city and living the good life, making money and spending time shopping, having fun and partying. So, who was I?

I realised that I cared about something that I'd forgotten about. If someone had told me, before I threw myself into the corporate rat race, that I could find my true path by *remembering who I was* as a child and rekindling some of those passions, then I might have developed a business and found fulfilment much earlier. That's not to say that time in employment was wasted. I believe those of us who have been employed by other people have learned much from those roles and from the organisations for which we've worked. We have gained the commercial acumen to enable us to build our own businesses, using larger business protocols as a template that we can use to develop our start-ups. I transferred a lot of the skills in my startup which I acquired in finance and logistics. I have an understanding of HR policies, company procedures and sales systems which I wrote straight into my joinery firm. This gave me the advantage over many of my competitors, who may never have experienced how a large, efficient organisation operates. This made it easier for my team to scale up.

Remembering who I was and what I actually cared about meant that I could return to England with a new understanding of myself. I knew that I wanted to do more with my life than go back to my career in finance.

Fortunately for you, your past and current work situation may not be as drastically out of alignment with your ideal future. You may not find that you have to take such extreme measures to design the business you are soon to create. I had lost my way. Forgotten who I was. Is this true for you too? Or are you already in a place where you know who you really are? Did you pick up this book feeling content with where you currently are or did it speak to you because you know, deep down, that there is something else waiting for you?

You may be in a position where starting again seems impossible (but I urge you to find the means necessary to do so) or you could perhaps side-step out of your present paid employment into another job in the industry in which you would like to start a business.

Let's begin at the beginning. Remember who you were when you were younger. Then let's project this forward to who you envision yourself to be in the future.

Only once you have gained an understanding of who and what you truly are, can you gain a clear vision of the type of life that will make you genuinely happy. Whatever you care about, let that be the basis for the choices you now make. If you need to leave your job and go back to college, please, do it. Yes, it's hard. Yes, you will suffer a financial setback for the first few years. But you will gain a life which is immeasurably different to what you have now. It's worth every penny you might lose in the short term.

As difficult as this might be for you to swallow, sometimes the only option is to stop what you're doing and start again. It is only then that a spark of inspiration can manifest into a sensational business or product that can then be acted upon. I can't give you your idea – like any lone warrior or knight heading out into battle, some things are yours to face alone. The journey of a start-up founder is both profoundly fulfilling and incredibly diverse but it will transport you to a place that is light years away from the people you know and love. Like shedding an old skin, you may seem noticeably different to those who've known you for a long time. This total realignment of mindset and perspective can unfortunately negatively impact your current relationships, so prepare yourself for the onslaught which will invariably come from others around you who might not share your vision. The naysayers and the 'concerned' friends and family members might try to discourage you from change. Ostensibly to protect you, but in reality, this is due to their own feelings of inadequacy and you cannot hope to change them without first helping yourself. It's hard to discount comments from those around you who are actively discouraging you from taking the leap. This is where you need to cultivate the warrior spirit! You may discover that you need to transition into a different tribe. New people will arrive in your life to support your next phase, but you may certainly lose others.

I'd like to suggest to you that there are three versions of 'you'. One is the you as you see yourself; second, is how others perceive you; and the third version is the one who you'd ultimately like to be. In fact, I'd go so far as to say that there's actually a fourth version. The person you are about to become, *the real you who has been hiding away* since early childhood and yet you are completely unaware of! These are all inextricably linked but are different in varying degrees.

There is a theory that true authenticity is reached when a person's thoughts, speech and actions are all in complete alignment. There is no contradiction. I was out of alignment when I had the Borneo experience. It was all of a sudden painfully evident that the 'me' wasn't 'me' at all. I'd gone off track somewhere down the line. I wonder, can you see any contradictions in your life?

BEGIN AT THE BEGINNING

Knowing yourself is the beginning of all wisdom.

Aristotle

Take a moment, right now, to sit and think about an alternative life. Project yourself into a parallel world. A perfect world where you are the most magnificent version of yourself. A picture-perfect, catalogue shot of you in your element. Living the best life you could possibly imagine.

What do you see? How would you carry yourself? Can you see any hobbies? Are there other people in the picture? How are you dressed? How and where would you be working and living? Are you fit and healthy? Does the picture you hold in your mind evoke any feelings? Joy, perhaps? Are you laughing? What's in the background? A dog? Are you at work in your vision? Perhaps at a desk at home or in a creative studio? Are you visualising a glamorous corner office in a city or a small workshop in the country... Put yourself in the centre of this visualisation. Feel it. Smile. Breathe into it. Be there. Focus on the highlights. What's the overall theme?

Have you got it? Great.

Because that's where you're going. Start making this your manifesto. Keep it in the forefront of your mind. Create your business idea around the person you are going to transform into. Bring yourself into alignment with where you are meant to be, not where you currently are.

For example, if you saw a clear image of yourself standing on a craggy hill, windswept and laughing, with a dog at your feet and a glow to your cheeks, then this would indicate that you need a business which suits an outdoors-based lifestyle or where you can work from home for a large part of the time, enabling you to get a dog and get outside at every opportunity. Start thinking about which hobbies could lead to potential business ideas.

What changes can you make, right now, to enable you to reach this ideal version of your life? What profession would enable you to relocate to a rural location?

If you have the time, please, I would like you to run through an exercise with me. Take a piece of plain paper, the bigger the better. Take some pens and start with these words in the middle of the page:

'My life – today'

Add the date. Draw a bubble around it and then, as quickly as you can, extend lines out from the bubble one at a time to create a spider diagram, and at the end of each line start throwing words down which indicate what your situation is and how you are feeling about it. All of the things you're dissatisfied with and you'd like to change.

An example could be:

Trapped in my current profession
Earning £-- per year
Miserable at work – I hate my boss
Not spending enough time with my family
Would like to see my friends more
Worried about my age/taking a new direction
Keep snapping at wife and kids – feeling angry
Wondering what I can do next
Frustrated by a current issue (insert your frustration here, plastics, pollution, education...)

Please, don't feel too disheartened. This is a starting point. Ground zero. The only way is up from here. Once you've brain-dumped all of your feelings and facts about where you are at this present moment it's time to move on to creating your new reality.

Take another piece of paper or flip over to the reverse of your bubble diagram and write in the centre, 'My ideal life'. Date it five years from now. As before, start working your way around the bubble with the visual scene you pictured in your 'dream life' scenario. Note down what you'd like to be earning, what you'd like to be doing in your spare time, how your friends and family might see you. Where you'd like to live.

Next, draw up a list of all of the things you love to do and start highlighting the activities that you love the most and what you think you're good at. Even better, make a note of the things you've not yet tried but *would like to learn*. Then you can navigate a way to find the career to align with these passions. You might discover something that sparks a whole new interest for you.

When I returned back to the UK in early 2007 I embarked on this process myself. When I came home I drifted around for a while, unsure of what to do next. Not wanting a corporate job, I dabbled in temp jobs, TV extra work, café work, bar work and anything non-linear. I was pretending to myself that I was 'still travelling' and I resisted the idea of going back to normal life for as long as possible. But I still didn't have an idea of what I wanted to do or who I could be. It was only after a few months that I realised I needed a proper salary and fell into a management role with a growing and successful UK mail order firm. Again, I fell back onto the hamster wheel and was earning a good salary but I knew, deep inside, that this wasn't going to help the jungles in Borneo.

It was after a late night drunken conversation with my best friend that I eventually recognised I needed a total career change. I'd been hiding from this. Pretending that I didn't need to change. I needed to start again.

It was through having the courage to stop and start all over again that becoming an entrepreneur became possible. And yet I still didn't realise what lay ahead.

I wrote down a list of all of the things I enjoyed, was interested in and what I saw in my 'dream life' scenario. In my imagination, my most magnificent version of myself would be enmeshed in art and design, the outdoors, music, great food and nutrition ... all of the things I take an interest in outside of 'work'.

Now I needed to create a career around these interests.

My initial passion was Nutrition. This is an emerging field with so many fascinating elements that touch every area of our lives. From a planetary perspective, our agricultural revolution has shaped the very surface of this planet in unimaginable ways. Our food system dictates the way the land is managed and it underpins the farming practices which can have a positive or detrimental effect on global and local wildlife. At the end of this process, the food produced has a phenomenal influence on our lives and the ultimate fascination for me was the effect that optimum nutrition might have on our NHS and personal health and wellbeing. From my perspective, it seemed to be both an alluring and incredibly satisfying profession that would benefit lives on an enormous scale while feeding my personal interests in the subject.

But, I wasn't yet an entrepreneur. I didn't yet understand how to follow my instincts and listen to my inner guidance. Entrepreneurship fosters and encourages these skills. I was, at that point, paralysed by indecision.

The two options eventually brought me to a total standstill. It was a decision that I eventually made on the advice of my 83-year-old grandmother, Esmee. When I came to her with my agonising decision of whether I study to become an interior designer or nutritionist she looked at me and simply asked: 'Well, which profession pays more?' Simple, I suppose.

I chose interior design. With hindsight, choosing a career for salary expectations alone is NOT the right way to approach a new profession or industry, but I didn't recognise this at the time. Taking career advice from someone who was born in 1925 is not something I would recommend either.

Ten years down this track, I have moved from design to eco-buildings, and now environmental conservation and organic farming on rural estates, schools and nature reserves. This is through the contacts I've made and the flexibility of the career I now have. I believe your path always finds you, eventually. There is no such thing as a wrong decision. Whatever you decide. You give it your all. It will lead you where you're meant to be.

The trick is to start out by first understanding what you're interested in and recognising where you might have come unstuck or hit the wrong track. How many negative self-beliefs are you holding onto which were placed upon you by adults when you were a child? Let's shatter them. Let's break down those walls and find out who you are so you can step out into the world as the most magnificent version of yourself. Because when you shine your light brightly, you give others permission to do the same. You owe it not only to yourself, but to everyone around you.

WHAT IS AN ENTREPRENEUR?

You don't build a business, you build people,
then people build the business.

Zig Ziglar

American author, salesman and motivational speaker

'So, I am self-employed. Doesn't that mean I'm an entrepreneur?' Not quite. From my perspective, there is an enormous difference between being a freelancer/self-employed professional and an entrepreneur. Put simply, a self-employed person secures work for themselves and is paid directly by their clients. Usually referred to as a 'sole trader', there is no legal distinction between the person and the business entity. Many self-employed professionals work in established industries (design, catering, photography etc.) and are working within the expectations and confines of that industry. Entrepreneurs, however, will create a new niche within a given industry or create a new industry altogether.

An entrepreneur creates something much larger than themselves. They visualise an end result and then they take steps to achieve it. Entrepreneurs actively change industries, innovate, create and expand markets. Bringing other people along on their journey. Entrepreneurs design a 'business' of varying complexity that usually brings a unique concept to industry. Most entrepreneurs design and build businesses that have (a) multiple members of staff on the payroll (b) an office address which isn't their home and (c) a product or service which has the potential to shape industry and disrupt the status quo. An entrepreneur is a pioneer, explorer and change-maker. I see entrepreneurs as problem-solvers and innovators. I see them as rebellious. Many activists create impact through entrepreneurial activities. The founders of many international and national charities and social enterprises are entrepreneurs. They seek to solve a systemic problem in our society or plug a gap in an otherwise untapped market. They can swiftly transition from one industry to another, irrespective of knowledge in that arena. Entrepreneurs create products, drive movements and affect people's lifestyles.

Usually, a sole-trader is the only person responsible for their venture and works to deliver the goods and services. They are locked in to a day-to-day grind of admin and customer service. An entrepreneur may own several businesses without necessarily needing to be involved in the day-to-day running of these ventures. The term 'businessman' usually refers to a business owner of a product or service which is not a new idea. An entrepreneur is a *market leader* whereas the businessman is a *market player.* Ironically, an entrepreneur will most likely be employed as opposed to self-employed once their venture is up and running, as Director/Founder of their own firm.

An excellent example of how one person can literally change the behaviour of our whole civilisation is Henry Ford. He is arguably one of the most recognised figures of industry. Without him, we may not have seen the emergence of the motor car as we know it.

What would have happened if Henry Ford had missed the opportunity to follow his interests and pursue his ideas? How might the world be different if he'd worked in a job for someone else and quietened his voice or ignored his interests? If he'd listened to the advice of his father he would have been a farmer. That was his destiny according to his autobiography. But Ford knew what he was interested in and focused on that. He fixated on his target. To create the engine.

Henry Ford writes in his autobiography: 'I was born on a farm in Michigan. From the beginning I could never work up much interest in farming. I wanted to have something to do with machinery. My father was not entirely in sympathy with my bent towards mechanics. He thought that I ought to be a farmer. When I became an apprentice I was all but given up for lost. When I passed my apprenticeship I worked nights in a jewellery shop. It was just about the time the standard railroad time was being arranged. Like the daylight saving days, the railroad time differed from the local time. That bothered me a great deal so I succeeded in making a watch that kept both times. It had two dials and was quite a curiosity in the neighbourhood.'

Henry Ford illustrates the mindset of an entrepreneur. He knew what he was interested in (mechanics) and he sought to solve problems (the difference in times) and used his newly acquired skills to create a new type of watch. He also shared the same problem many of us will recognise. His father wanted him to be a farmer and offered him very little encouragement to pursue a career in anything else.

At the age of just 16, before his apprenticeship, Ford had long harboured the idea of making a light steam car that would take the place of the horses on the farm. He writes: 'I felt perfectly certain that horses, considering all the bother attending them and the expense of feeding, did not earn their keep. The obvious thing to do was to design and build a steam engine that would be light enough to run an ordinary wagon or pull a plough. It was circumstances that took me first into the actual manufacture of road cars. I found eventually that people were more interested in something that would travel on the road than in something that would do work on the farms.'

As with Ford, if you want to become an entrepreneur, you must look towards identifying what the public actually needs rather than what you, the creator might *think* they need. Designing a business around the consumer means creating something of value to those who are willing to spend money on it instead of designing something you wish to make money from and then trying to convince people to buy it.

Realising that people were more interested in motor cars than ploughing machines, Ford quickly switched his focus.

It was the foundation of the motor car business of his career. This is what we call 'pivoting' in the world of start-up culture.

But when Ford hit the age of 24, his father offered him forty acres of timber land, provided he gave up being a machinist. Ford set up a sawmill and did as his father asked. But after three years, he left and ended up back in mechanics, working in the day for an electrical company and then using his nights and weekends experimenting with motors and engines. But for him, it wasn't hard work. He stated that, 'I cannot say that it was hard work. No work with interest is ever hard. I am always certain of results. They always come if you work hard enough. I had to work from the ground up. That is, although I knew that a number of people were working on horseless carriages, I could not know what they were doing.' At the age of 30, in 1893, Ford had completed his first motor car. It had taken a year from first completion to the point that it ran to his satisfaction:

> 'My 'Gasoline Buggy' was the first, and for a long time the only auto mobile in Detroit. It was considered to be something of a nuisance, for it made a racket and it scared horses. Also, it blocked traffic. For if I stopped my machine anywhere in town, a crowd was around it before I could start up again. Even if I left it alone for a minute, some inquisitive person always tried to run it. Finally, I had to carry a chain and chain it to a lamp-post whenever I left it anywhere. And then there was trouble with the police. I do not know quite why, for my impression is that there were no speed-limit laws in those days. Anyway, I had to get a special permit from

> the mayor and thus for a time enjoyed the distinction of being the only licensed chauffeur in America. I ran that machine about one thousand miles through 1895 and 1896 and then sold it for two hundred dollars. This was my first sale. I had built the car not to sell, but only to experiment with. I wanted to start another car. I could use the money and we had no trouble in agreeing upon a price.'

So, what did Henry Ford feel about business and what were the lessons learnt?

> 'There is a great fear of being thought a fool. So many men are afraid of being considered fools. I grant that public opinion is a powerful influence for those who need it. But it is not a bad thing to be a fool for righteousness' sake. The best of it is that such fools usually live long enough to prove that they were not fools – or the work they have begun lives long enough to prove that they were not foolish.'

Entrepreneurs all start from a place of doubt. Most swim against the tide. All of them fail at some point or another but continue onwards with the tenacity of a warrior. Sadly, a vast majority of us have been conditioned to believe that we can never become the next Henry Ford. Even Henry Ford himself was pushed by his father to be something other than a mechanic or engineer. He could all too easily have given up on his dreams and succumbed to the life of farming. How steadfast he had been in his convictions that he pushed ahead anyway. He couldn't have possibly known that his name is now synonymous with the automotive industry. We are told to be realistic with our ambitions and thus conditioned to believe that there is stability in the very things that (I believe) are not particularly stable. A paid job is not stable. Your employer could go bankrupt or close their business at any point. Our financial system is not stable. The banks can go bankrupt. Our healthcare system is not stable and pharmaceuticals are not serving us as well as they could. Sadly, prescription drugs are all too often taken with many side effects outweighing the benefits they are intended to provide. But, do we question them as much as we should? No.

Because we act and we believe as we are told. It has been this way since we were small children. If you could unlearn what you've been taught about 'stability' then you might find the courage to do as Ford did and be prepared to look like a fool for the sake of doing what is right for you. Certainly, he must have looked crazy to others when he was working away through the evenings and weekends in his workshop – like a mad professor obsessing over a 'big idea'. Getting into trouble with the police, holding up the traffic and chaining his first prototype to lamp-posts. This must've put Ford in a predicament where he was publicly making a very real but crude attempt at something that, much later, became one of the most recognisable businesses and inventions of all time. What would Henry Ford look like in today's society? I would imagine he could be very much like you or I. Working a day job, spending his evenings experimenting with a personal hobby. But determination and a laser-like focus on his end result took him to exactly where he wanted to go.

Entrepreneurs often take the shape of a free-thinker who has discovered their true interests and thus are using their time and energy to bring something new to the table. They have noticed a problem that needs solving and they are using their thoughts and energy to generate new ideas and new concepts that assist with shaping our society. Are you a free thinker?

THE WORLD NEEDS YOUR IDEAS

A man may die, nations may rise and fall,
but an idea lives on.

J. F. Kennedy

I personally believe that the real reason to start a business is not to make money. It's to create products and services that make the world a better place. The money is secondary, an indicator of a job well done. Your project, if successful, will bring you the financial security and professional credibility that no employer ever could.

But, if you were interested in the money element, let me tell you this. As an employee, you have one resource that you're selling to your employer. Your time. You are a single human resource. Your revenue (salary) is dictated by your employer.

Aside from any supplementary benefit you may gain as a bonus, private healthcare, sales commission, and so on, the ceiling to your annual earnings is fixed by an external factor.

As an entrepreneur, however, you are playing an entirely different game. You are selling a concept, a product, a service, a movement, a philosophy AND your time. Your revenue is limited only by the market and your business's performance, and your salary is completely irrelevant if you are sitting on a company worth hundreds of thousands or millions of pounds.

Everything that you are surrounded by has been designed, manufactured and distributed by the minds of our fellow men and women. So what if I told you that you can be an active participant in this creation process? It's time for you to decide whether you are a creator or a consumer.

Some might say that it's the governments and big corporations who run the world. Yes, governments have their place. To govern. To regulate. To manage and monitor. However, the real innovation, the true movement of our civilisation, comes from the average person. The entrepreneur, attributes of whom we all have inside us. Creativity is the cornerstone of the human spirit. It's creativity which presents ideas to you through your imagination.

We live in an age of capitalism. Products are produced, consumers buy them. Services and experiences are created, consumers pay for them. Taxes are paid and they go to the government, but our governments do not create the markets, products and services. We do. It's up to us. You are part of this whether you like it or not. You can shield yourself from this reality if you like, cover your eyes, put this book down, and go back to feeding the machine. Or, you can wake up to the fact that the machine is being built, piece by piece, by people just like you and me. You are here to contribute, and to help it evolve into a system that is ready for the next generation. We need you. You have no idea how important it is to me and the rest of the world that you answer that call and accept that you could in fact be an entrepreneur.

Some, like Anita Roddick at the Body Shop or Steve Jobs at Apple are well recognised for their contributions, and their influence and ideas will be remembered long after their death.

So too, can yours. You are needed and you are valuable.

Whatever your earlier career path or academic achievements, you have built up a wealth of knowledge and valuable life skills which you can transform into a venture. The best part? It's never been easier to access information and to create a business. You can easily find the resources necessary to take the step towards recreating and rebuilding our system. With the internet as your endless resource, you have connectivity to mentors, seminars, books, TED Talks of inspirational speakers, business coaches, finance packages, free legal advice online, business plan templates. It's all there. You just have to get yourself motivated and start your research.

Many of the products and services we use were created with an old way of thinking and without the knowledge and insight we have today. The men who led the industrial revolution were shaping our society over 100 years ago. Those designers, engineers, architects, innovators, and entrepreneurs all lived in a world that was entirely different to our contemporary reality. There were just *one billion* people living on the planet in 1800. At the time of writing this, there are currently 7.9 billion human inhabitants on earth. The rules have changed.

Several generations ago, creators of their time were inventing plastics, combustion engines, pharmaceuticals and the financial system. All of these were created to serve a purpose of their time and created with a mindset of a different world-view. All of these concepts and systems have been outgrown by our present day society and they are causing more harm than good in many ways. We need a fresh way of thinking, rooted in the present day, by people living normal lives. People like you.

The entrepreneurs who founded our industries had little or no regard for climate change, carbon emissions, microplastics, deforestation, excessive consumerism, devastating habitat depletion, western obesity crisis, the coronavirus pandemic and spiralling mental health issues. Alarmingly, industry is not moving as quickly as the growth of consumer knowledge and we must mobilise quickly to accommodate the shifting demands of the informed consumer.

You are part of the solution. It's your life experience and your perspective which could play a part in solving the problems we collectively face. If we design useful products that replace or eliminate the need for the damaging ones, then that's a step in the right direction. If we create services that enrich the lives of others, then that's a step in the right direction. If we start designing a better world from the bottom up, then that's true everlasting change for our whole world. This starts with you. You and me. All of us. Real people. Entrepreneurs are not the flashy, multi-billionaires who appear in the media, flying around on private jets and lounging in their mansions. (Well, a few are but they are the exception!) Over 99% of all businesses in the UK are small to medium-sized enterprises, employing fewer than 250 people. Real entrepreneurs are *real people*. You may believe we are powerless to make any real change in the world, but we as small business owners represent 99% of the market. We have unimaginable power to shape our society through the goods we design, the services we provide and the solutions we bring. And the bonus? You get to gain total control of your life and financial freedom to boot – what's not to like?

Hanna Sillitoe, founder of 'My Goodness Recipes', a female entrepreneur, successful *Dragons' Den* contestant and influencer with 50,000 Instagram followers and a hugely popular wellness brand, explains how she came across her idea following on from profound long-term issues with her skin.

'Skin conditions had always plagued my life. Whatever turmoil was going on internally reflected on the outside. My skin was crying out for help. Red, flaky, painful patches of psoriasis and eczema covered my arms and tummy. Every part of my body itched and ached. My doctor wanted me on a chemotherapy drug in order to suppress my immune system to stop it from over-reacting. I realised then that I'd hit rock bottom and enough was enough.

'Once I'd set my mind on prioritising health, I got fully focused on making changes. My diet was the first thing to get an overhaul. I ditched the alcohol, cigarettes and junk food. Instead I drank freshly pressed green juice, switched to platefuls of plant-based ingredients and began exercising again. Within a month these dramatic changes in lifestyle began reflecting in my skin. Angry patches of eczema started to fade, I was sleeping better than ever, it felt like a huge fog was lifting and I had a clarity I'd never experienced before.

'I'd lived with awful skin for the best part of twenty years, and no medication had ever made me feel or look this good! I began enthusiastically blogging about my experience, hoping someone somewhere might read it and be inspired to make changes too. Soon I began receiving emails from all over the world – Sweden, Malaysia, the Netherlands – girls with similar skin issues seeing the same dramatic improvements through copying the simple changes I was blogging about. "You should write a book," a friend suggested.

I hadn't realised it at the time, but I'd already started building my skincare business.

'I'd never written a book before, but the words just seemed to flow and the process felt cathartic.

My mission was to help others make dietary and lifestyle changes to heal their skin.

'"How do you think I go about publishing this?" I was sat with Rachel at the breakfast bar in her kitchen. She didn't know, so we googled "how to publish a book".

'The obvious starting point would be approaching a publisher, but it seems that's not the done thing. First you have to get yourself a literary agent, then *they* approach publishers. We emailed a handful of seemingly relevant agencies. "Expect to wait four to six weeks for a response," said the advice online. I'm not a naturally patient person, so this wait was going to be tough. As it turned out I needn't have worried. Within less than a day I'd got a reply, then two, then three.

'I never wrote *Radiant* to make me any money. As an entrepreneur, that might sound a little strange, but writing had become part of my self-care plan to keep me accountable and on track. I posted regularly on Instagram, to motivate myself as much as others.

'The social media following grew naturally and organically. This was such an odd concept to me. I wasn't having to spend money on advertising, I wasn't posting content with the sole purposes of drumming up new business, people were genuinely interested in the information I was sharing. I began receiving questions about running workshops and courses. Sure, I thought. Why not?

'My passion for health and wellness thrived. I loved sharing everything I'd learned and making a real difference to people's lives. I began hosting online seminars, weekend workshops and eventually my first health retreat in Croatia. "If only I could make *this* my life," I said wistfully to a friend. "Well, do so!" he said.

'The cosmetics market is notoriously tough. There are millions of skincare products. I'd transitioned to using much more raw and natural ingredients such as coconut oil and mineral salts on my own skin. The bit I did struggle with was my hair. Shop-bought shampoos made my scalp itch like crazy, and nothing natural I'd found so far seemed to do a decent job of washing it properly.

'A friend of a friend recommended a local aromatherapist. "This lady makes her own skincare," she said, "It's really good." We set up a meeting. Could she make me a shampoo, I asked. 100% natural but actually effective. She assured me she could. She did and I loved it! And so my haircare range came to be.

'Haircare expanded into skincare. We developed serums and balms, all with the primary purpose of naturally soothing sore skin. It didn't sell by the thousands, but I managed to sell a handful of bottles each week to cover the bills. I wasn't earning anywhere near what I'd been making a year or two earlier, but I loved helping people and having the time to look after myself properly.

'Over the past eighteen months we've significantly expanded the skincare range, developed a best-selling probiotic vitamin. I've written a second book and launched a juice cleanse delivery service. The passion for my work and what I do grows stronger day by day. I still love to travel in my camper, I enjoy the freedom of adventure, but no longer feel a desperate urge to run away. The beauty of continually growing and developing my own business full of passion and purpose is that I have absolutely no idea what the next eighteen months have in store. I can't wait to find out!'

IF WOMEN ROSE...

If we're not changing, we're not learning
and we're not growing.

Sharon Blackie
writer, psychologist, mythologist

Making the decision to radically change your life and become an entrepreneur is deeply fulfilling on an emotional level but will require you to change yourself in ways you may find unimaginable at first. You may reflect that you were seemingly happier when you were blissfully unaware of your purpose and your skills remained underutilised. Just like I was when working in finance. I *thought* I was happy! But, on reflection, I was asleep. I wasn't contributing anything to society, I was just creating a lifestyle for myself and following orders from my employer. When the time came to make the change, I had to put measures in place to enable me to step out of the world of work which I knew and in which I felt comfortable, to embark into a new sector which I knew absolutely nothing about.

My start-up journey commenced the moment I decided to actively switch careers at the age of 28. Soon after returning from my Borneo adventure which preceded the two year residency in New Zealand, I begrudgingly took a nine-to-five job in an office as a manager for a mail order firm. The boss, an Iranian chap called 'Payman' was ambitious and hard working. His firm, started as a market stall ten years before, was well on its way to becoming a national brand. Having a growing team of staff and revenues creeping up to £1m, he was pushing to be the next Argos. The plans were huge. But, I knew I wanted to be a designer, attain freedom and build my own business. So, I started studying on an interior design night course at a local college. I was determined to get the skills I needed to escape. Once I completed night school, I handed in my resignation and stepped towards my goal. I needed to become a full-time student for two years to complete the Commercial Diploma in Spatial Design. Once attained, I'd be qualified as an interior designer for industry, capable of designing airport lounges, restaurants, hotels and other commercial spaces. Fast-tracking into an architectural degree, if I wished to continue. I was determined to make my break. My boss looked at me aghast when I told him I had to leave to follow my dreams as a designer. He considered me completely insane and offered me every perk in the company including a position as a co-director, car and increased salary. When that didn't work, he sat me down and worked hard to convince me that being a designer is a tough career and I probably wouldn't make it.

'Gemma,' he sighed, waving my letter of resignation in the air and gesturing to a seat opposite his lavishly polished wooden desk in his enormous corner office. I took my seat, reluctantly.

'You have a great career here. I think you're making a mistake. Listen, I'll make you a partner, we'll drive this business forward. I'm not sure why you think design is a good option. My sister-in-law is an interior designer – it's a terrible life!!!' (He rolled his eyes for theatrical effect.) 'She's always pitching for work and working through the night for crazy deadlines; always up against so many other designers and architects. Please, reconsider. It's not that you can't dream, or have a hobby, but your career is here. You know it is...' He looked at me in such a reassuring way, and I immediately felt a pang of regret. But it wasn't enough to dispel my ambition for my new life. Creating something of value was dominating my thoughts. He was being kind, genuine, and clearly a rational businessman who foresaw the success which lay ahead with his firm. Nowadays, his firm has skyrocketed and is a market leader. He was absolutely right about the opportunity he was offering me.

But, an entrepreneur seeks freedom. Always. This, my friend, is where you need to remain strong – paid employment in anything other than your dream is not acceptable. Resisting all offers of a secure life and against the advice of most 'rational' people who knew me, I went back to school.

Those three years of transition and learning were absolutely worthwhile. Becoming a designer forced me to switch off the left, analytical side of my brain and tune into the right, creative side of the brain. Put simply, I just couldn't draw or illustrate to scale at all when I started studying. Through the course work and patience of tutors I was encouraged to keep trying. They asked me to study the forms of nature, look at the world in an interested way, think of colours and textures in a way I'd not noticed previously. Before too long, slowly and incrementally, I started to see the world differently. With it, the skills required to draw, envisage and create were gradually unearthed. Who'd have thought it? Moreover, the skills to find solutions appeared. With creativity, comes problem-solving!

Problem-solving through creativity is the cornerstone of entrepreneurship. Entrepreneurs are creatives. I would argue that we are all born with creativity, but we lose it when we go to school. As with any muscle, it needs practice to get back into shape. So if you are working in a non-creative field but want to become an entrepreneur I would absolutely recommend you take a creative night class. Pottery, art, poetry, music, anything which encourages creativity will greatly benefit you. Learning to create literally rewires your brain and enables you to think in a way in which you hadn't before. It also gives you practice in hyper-focus. When I am creating a piece of artwork or a model or even this book, I focus for hours on end. This form of focus in a world where we're constantly interrupted by smartphones and attention-sapping distractions is a skill that's worth cultivating. Hyper-focus is a superpower.

My advice to you here is to get started in the general direction of where you want to go. Then let the path weave and wind and lead you to your specialism within that field. Whether you make the right choice or not, stepping forward in *any* direction which is away from where you are now is a very positive move. If you've made your list of interests and skills, and visualised yourself in the dream scenario then you may discover, as you move forward into the new direction, that there is more than one business opportunity waiting to be activated when the time (and the markets) are right.

My experience of Borneo may have awoken my inner spirit, but it hadn't fully woken me to the possibility of the life I now live. I still do regular bubble diagrams and visualisations similar to the ones we went through in the earlier chapters. You will find that the dream scenario changes year-on-year, each one becoming more and more in focus with the person you are capable of becoming.

I didn't know it at the time, but by taking action and starting a college course I had made a significant step towards the future in which I am now living. This culminated with one life-affirming experience which set me on the course for my future career as an entrepreneur. That one decision to switch industry led me *directly* to Aidan and then catapulted me on to the Pinewood Studio floor, facing five titans of industry. All within two years.

While I was a student, I was told by one of my tutors that the secret to getting the job you want is to find the company you want to work with and approach them directly. This worked for me, and it could work for you too. It might help you to learn about an industry before you plunge into building your own business in that sector. A huge percentage of vacancies aren't even advertised and if you happen to catch the right person at the right time, there is no telling what you could achieve. And remember, offering work for free is absolutely essential in some cases.

This is why I urge you. Please. Step away from the work you are currently doing if you are not jumping out of bed each morning eager to get started. Your life is too short to be working away to facilitate someone else's dream. The mean boss, the co-workers who gossip behind your back, the uneasy feeling you have in the pit of your stomach? These are ENORMOUS red flags! Get out, while you can. What must you let go of in order to be truly, genuinely happy? Can you accept that you'll experience a temporary set-back and lose some short-term benefits for the long-term project which is – the rest of your life?

Why now, and why you? Look around, dear feminine. The world is like a teenager gone off the rails. Dad has been running the show and he's been drunk on power with his buddies for several hundred years. It's time for the feminine to intervene. To gently nurture it back on track. Before we lose it all, forever. We might have taken our chance to help build a better kind of industry in the Middle Ages if we weren't burnt at the stake and accused of witchcraft. Those of us with the will to create something new, the burning indignation at witnessing such corruption, and the ability to work on a *better* way of doing business are the next wave of strong women. The last group of women who formed a radical movement like this were the suffragettes. They came together and got things done. This is what we must do. We'll do this by generating great ideas and build businesses which elevate us all. You have to make a choice, my dear. Would you like to be a creator or a consumer? Do you hear the call?

Sharon Blackie, mythologist and psychologist, author of *If Women Rose Rooted* writes, 'The call comes when we break, or are ready to break. Sometimes it may come in the form of a change of circumstances: a relationship ends, we lose our job, we become ill. A child leaves home; a loved one dies. Sometimes the call comes to us in a dream.'

Sharon writes about feminism, culture, mythology and the environment. She articulates her frustration at the male-dominated industrial world which we all inhabit and echoes the philosophy of this book when she writes that, 'The world which men made isn't working. Something needs to change. To change the world, we women need first to change ourselves – and then we need to change the stories we tell about who we are. The stories we've been living by for the past few centuries. Stories matter, you see. They're not just entertainment – stories matter because humans are narrative creatures. It's not simply that we like to tell stories, and to listen to them: it's that narrative is hard-wired into us. It's a function of our biology, and the way our brains have evolved over time. We make sense of the world and fashion our identities through the sharing and passing on of stories. For women particularly, to have a Celtic identity or ancestry is to inherit a history, literature and mythology in which we are portrayed not only as connected to the natural world but as playing a unique and critical role in the well-being of the earth and survival of its inhabitants.'

Sharon speaks for all of us. Her plea is that we rise up into the world as aspirational, intentional beings, all the while rooted to the earth, like a tree. Grounded, stable and strong. The world around us has been shaped by capitalism. Men's capitalism. We are part of the zeitgeist of growth and consumerism. But what if we all collectively rose up and took our places in this churning industrial chessboard and positioned our pieces with grit and determination to claim financial security whilst delivering heart-led solutions which reflect the positive change we seek to make? As a nurturing feminine, we might just steer the ship in a more positive direction. You see, Sharon reflects in her book that women, historically, were respected as the guardians of the land. In our Celtic history, women were responsible for interpreting and protecting the wishes of the earth and its inhabitants. As I write this, in 2023, I feel that we are needed. All of us. The earth is calling us. If a million women, like you and I, created our businesses which brought about positive change, protection and innovation, we might have a fighting chance of transforming the system, from the inside.

I can only draw this conclusion from my own experience and the reason I know it to be true is because I saw the difference my business made to the world. In just ten years, I brought the ancient roundhouse back to the British Isles. As a contemporary interpretation, yes, but the spirit of our ancestors resided in those designs. 130 of them are built across the country, as far south as Cornwall and Kent, and as far north as the Outer Hebrides. Many are straddling ley lines and on sites where ancient roundhouses once stood. I often wondered why my business was so different to anyone else's in industry. Working in the masculine world of timber-framed construction, the market was awash with rectangular garden rooms and school classrooms. But my project was so different. I was designing circular buildings. Everyone else was designing square. Why is this? Because I am a woman? Because I care? Because I have seen the disappearing jungles of Borneo and Indonesia or simply because I saw something that everyone else missed?

Personally, I think it's because I applied the laws of nature to my business. When you create from a place of reverence for the natural world, you can't help but integrate it. Being a woman, I seemed to attract other women. All of my clients, for the first five years of trading, without exception, were women. I find that remarkable. We recognise each other through our work.

This, my friend, is why I am writing from the heart, as one woman to another. Because I took the risk and travelled the path of the start-up founder, I know the power of creative entrepreneurship. I can understand now, how an idea can become a prototype, a prototype a sale, a client transform into a pipeline, and a dreamer into an entrepreneur. Having built my unique business in a male-dominated industry.

Consequently, it shone brightly, it blazed a trail; because it was different to anything any man had thought to produce.

My buildings were unique, natural, outrageously simple and considerate. A circle. It's not so hard to imagine, is it? When you're a woman, that is. I have absolutely no idea why I was the first in the UK to create roundhouses on a national scale but I can only imagine that my perspective is unique, and as such, my business reflected that.

I often joked about how absurd it was to be starting out as an eco-building designer in an industry dominated by male architects and builders. They were furiously constructing their millions of timber boxes and rectangles and competing against each other; whilst I was forging ahead, alone, with my unique little circles. But, that's what defined my early success. I didn't have any competitors. It was a totally new concept. That's what will define your success too. The courage to stand alone, to stand rooted, in an ocean of what industry perceives to be 'normal', and to bring a unique gift to the world. Unique because only you can see the world in the way in which you do. This is your strength. This is what will define you.

So, why you? Because you, like me, are hungry for change. You're determined to make a financial success of yourself, but you are passionate enough to want to do this by creating something beautifully and authentically you. This is wonderfully refreshing. Above all else, you are a warrior. You can make a huge success of your life without compromising on ethics, and lead with integrity and with pride. You are a woman of the earth – playing the game of capitalism and harnessing it to create a life of your dreams, and a business which will bring joy and happiness to others without destroying the planet. To safeguard your children and grandchildren from the ever growing monolithic threat of corporations and big business. To create a new type of business. Heart-led. Earth-led. It's what I like to call Compassionate Capitalism.

What's more, the more joyful, practical and helpful your solution to others, the more money you stand to make. It's a battle you have no intention of losing. I believe that the animals and creatures of this planet are waiting on you, too. You are a woman of the land, and our land needs us to rise. If the land could speak, she'd ask you to break into the machine. Get inside it. Inspect the mechanisms. It's broken. It's churning out more damage day by day. If you can repair or replace one harmful cog with a harmless one, you'll be rewarded with a lifestyle and financial security which will make it worth your while.

OPPORTUNITIES ARE EVERYWHERE

The morning of Wednesday, 12 May 2009 changed my life forever. I drove up to a set of steel industrial gates at a small joinery and fabrication workshop on a farm in the outskirts of South Manchester. The gates opened out to a rough gravel parking area flanked by two low corrugated iron lean-to building units to my right. Ahead, fresh green crops growing in fields that stretched out to a hedgerow in the distance. I could hear the clatter of manufacturing and the whirr of circular saws from inside the units beside me. A quick scan of the car park revealed a building site with piles of materials everywhere, old car parts, trailers, vans, stacks of timber and steel bars, and metal storage containers dotted around the perimeter. There was an old caravan in the distance and a few chickens clucking about on the verge beside the fields. To the left, adjacent to the green fields, were monstrously large alien forms, rising up from the ground. Strange space-age buildings. Enormous house-sized domes. Only recognisable as a house due to the large oak front door set into a porch and wooden or plastic circular porthole windows dotted along the perimeter. Two of these great, reddish-coloured domes were connected together by a small corridor. I felt like I'd just landed on an eerie and atmospheric Dr Who film set and I was quite sure that, any moment, I might witness a Dalek or two, trundling out from behind one of those weird domes. 'Exterminaaaaaate!!!'

The external material was a terracotta rubber slate. These were flexible enough to mould to the curve of the walls, giving it a glossy egg-shaped appearance. The largest of the two pods must have been about 20 ft high. The width of the two connected structures was immense. Its sweeping curved walls swept down in a shallow arc to the decking area which followed the circumference of the building around the outside edge. Sitting across the yard from the big, connected domes was another structure, a tall rocket-shaped building. Graphite grey, wider at the bottom than the top, with a front door and porthole windows ... it was so tall ... momentarily I was blinded by the sheer audacity of it. A spaceship house. What was this madness?

The other students and the course leader were all gathered around in the car park, talking excitedly to one of the workmen on site. We were out of luck; the innovator behind the project, Aidan Quinn, was not around to see us. But we were told we could have a look inside the building anyway and read through the literature he had made available. I was the last person to step inside. Entering the strange, dome-shaped structure was a unique and uplifting sensation. I was immediately struck by how the smooth plastered walls wrapped around me, and the furniture curved and hugged the internal walls in one fluid, sweeping line. The arc of the walls swept up to a central point in the ceiling to where beams of sunlight shone in through a circular skylight window at the apex. It was like being in an egg-shaped, light-filled cave. It was astonishing. The interior furniture was constructed from plywood and in the living room sat a collection of second-hand armchairs and grey carpet tiles. Whoever designed these structures was clearly an engineer and not an interior designer, I thought. Leaflets on the kitchen counter proclaimed this building to be an 'Eco-Hab'.

This, I discovered, was short for 'Ecological Habitation'. The dome was designed as an eco-friendly alternative to the traditional home, 'saving up to 90% of a home's energy requirements', the leaflets stated. I knew very little about eco-buildings at the time but from what I could gather the dome home was super energy-efficient, needed very little in terms of heating, and required fewer materials to build than a traditional house. I stood in the centre of this dome, beneath the skylight and my internal compass was spinning wildly. I found the structures hugely exciting. Was this the future of human habitation on this planet? Eco-Pods?! Dome homes?!

I drove home that day elated, crazed and upbeat. My music was on full blast and I think I broke every speed limit as I careered wildly down the motorway. I was completely and unapologetically, in love. My head, whirring with possibilities and ignited by the idea of these weird and wonderful eco-pods. From the very moment I had stood under that dome and felt the electric buzz on my skin of sheer delight and wonder, I was in another world. The concept of a strange spaceship-shaped house with little porthole windows was utterly captivating. There was only one thing on my mind.

I wanted to work for this company more than anything in the world.

TAKE BOLD AND DECISIVE ACTION

The ultimate secret to growth is finding something worth fighting for.

Brendon Burchard

'We're not recruiting, sorry. I wish I could help, but...' The Irish inventor, Aidan, peered apologetically at me as I stood nervously in the doorway of his office.

I'd phoned him following our class visit and asked to meet him and ask a few questions, because I had missed him on the visit.

As I stood there clutching my portfolio of college assignments, I desperately sought an angle that would assist me with getting a foot in the door. 'How about I redesign the interior of your pods?' I suggested, pulling out some interior sketches and handing him some fabric swatches from my portfolio folder. 'Erm, no, it's fine thank you, I don't need interior designers.' He was clearly not interested. 'But what about some graphics?' I pleaded. Trying not to look too desperate (though I most certainly was). 'I can do graphic design...' I trailed off. Now I am not a particularly great graphic designer but I was willing to try anything to get into this organisation. 'I have a graphic designer, thank you.' He was not giving in easily.

'Listen, I'll work for free!' The words just cascaded out of my mouth before I'd even realised I'd spoken them.

Aidan stepped out from behind his desk and walked around it to get to the door of the joinery workshop. I turned on my heel and followed him outside where he was putting together some display boards. 'I can make scale models!' I declared, as a last and final plea just as he was walking away from me. 'Do you have any events coming up which would require one?' Aidan turned and looked me straight in the eye. He was a unique character. With bright blue eyes, wild grey hair and faded blue jeans coated in paint, glues and resins. His checked shirt was covered in sawdust. A bona fide inventor. 'As it so happens,' he started, in his rich but soft Irish accent, 'there is something I'm working on...'

He reached out to grasp two grey dome-shaped bowls sitting on a workbench. They were the size of basketballs. 'I'm making some scale models,' he added. 'I was planning on printing the graphics on some vinyl and wrapping these. D'ya think you could make something of them?' He handed one of the domes to me. From what I could tell, the form was made from a sanded-down fibreglass. They were the right shape but they were just a shell. Not dissimilar to when you break open an Easter egg along the seam down the middle to create a perfect half. I looked at them, turning them over in my hands, my thoughts whirring as I was imagining how I could make wooden slates out of balsa wood. For windows, a Fimo-type modelling clay with a finish similar to the one he had on the real structures. The window on the roof? Oh heck, I'd cut a circle from a fizzy drinks bottle...

'I can make these for you, Aidan,' I said. 'With windows, a door, the slates...' I looked across at him. 'When did you need it by?'

'Monday,' he said, flatly. 'For an exhibition in London.'

Oh crap. It was Friday.

I rushed out of his workshop as quickly as I'd arrived and flung myself and the two grey bowls into my little car, turned the ignition and sped away, sending the gravel flying. Exhilarated and terrified in equal measure, I had just two days to create a masterpiece and win him over. I needed the job; this was my way in.

I am a person who loves to sleep. But, that weekend I worked late into the night, falling into bed at 1 a.m. with my alarm set for 6 a.m. so I could get back to the scale model. Yes, it was crazy. I was doing this for free. I was sleep-deprived and

I was half-awake but I was determined and fuelled with a passion I'd not experienced before.

From my perspective, it was just another college assignment, only this was one which could land me the job of my dreams at the end of it. I had collected materials from the art shop on the way home from Eco-Hab and I had locked myself in my room from Friday afternoon until late Sunday evening. It was excruciatingly difficult to peel myself away from it to work my shift on Saturday evening at the restaurant. I was determined to finish this model. I cancelled every other commitment and didn't stop until I'd finished. Little did I know that a year or so later it would be on set with me in *Dragons' Den*.

Was I giving up my time and energy for something which, deep in my subconscious, I knew would pay dividends in the future? Who knows. I didn't recognise it on a conscious level. But, I learnt something from that experience. It's worth working (a) for free and (b) under immense pressure if it is an investment in the rest of your life.

Sunday evening came and I was attaching the last tile onto the model with super glue. My eyes were itchy and my fingers sore from working with the scalpel knife, cutting little squares of balsa and painting them with watercolour. I'd finally made it. It wasn't perfect, it certainly wasn't a masterpiece, but it resembled an Eco-Hab and I was ready to take it back to Aidan.

The journey towards being an actual entrepreneur began for me the very same day I brought the model back to Aidan. As I staggered out of my car, tired and broken, I slowly and carefully lifted the scale model out of the boot and walked across the gravel to Aidan's office-pod.

Thankfully, he was visibly delighted with his model and most likely relieved that I even came back at all. In return for the work I'd just presented to him, he offered me some work alongside him for a few days at the exhibition.

The following day, I was sitting on a train on my way down to London. Dressed in my smartest work clothes and reading the Eco-Hab literature, cover to cover. Absorbing as much as I could about the construction and benefits of these strange-looking buildings. Three days of standing at an exhibition and communicating with the general public about dome-shaped eco-buildings was not what I'd envisaged doing that week. Only a few days prior to this, I'd had no idea this firm existed. How amazing that life can change like that, in the blink of an eye or on the introduction of a new piece of information.

The three days at the Grand Designs exhibition as a representative of Eco-Hab was an experience which threw me fully out of my comfort zone and into a place of total confusion. Hundreds of people must have asked me questions I was perfectly incapable of answering, but somehow I managed to give Aidan the breathing space he needed to deal with one person at a time. Over the course of the exhibition I learnt a great deal about eco-buildings and developed a passion for this industry that has remained with me to this day. Aidan was a hilariously funny character and spoke with charm, confidence and knowledge when questioned about his invention.

From that point, the course of my life had been galvanised in exactly the direction I'd hoped it would. If I hadn't made that call, hadn't begged for work, hadn't worked for free or believed in a new path, I honestly don't think I would have founded a sensational joinery business and gained the experience and freedom that comes with it to write this book.

FORTUNE FAVOURS THE BRAVE

I learned that courage was not the absence of fear, but the triumph over it.

Nelson Mandela

I was not yet an entrepreneur when I appeared on *Dragons' Den*. But, I had graduated from college and started working full time as a Director of Eco-Hab Homes and O-Pod Buildings. I worked around the clock, keen to prove myself. Excited to have the opportunity to be assisting Aidan, I was euphoric from the moment I woke up until the minute I went to bed. To be part of this business was *literally a dream come true.*

Prior to meeting Aidan, I'd booked a once-in-a-lifetime trip to Costa Rica. Over the course of the past year, I'd saved up my student loans and earnings from my waitressing job to fulfil an ambition and face a personal fear, to travel as a backpacker, alone, to a non English-speaking country. Costa Rica is the most biodiverse country on the planet. I dreamt of this trip for many months as I trawled the internet, gazing at images of loggerhead turtles emerging from the ocean, hauling their heavy shells up from the tideline with their long, strong fins, on stretches of golden sandy beach fringed with tropical rainforests. I imagined the jungle canopy laden with many chattering scarlet macaws, lazy three-toed sloths and playful spider monkeys. It's a dramatic landscape of smouldering volcanoes, deep mist-shrouded rainforests, vibrant green cattle ranches and a rich Latin American culture.

I booked it knowing that I'd always felt that I could never do backpacking alone and it terrified me. So I wanted to mark the end of my student days and the arrival of my third decade with an adventure to build my confidence and spend time in tropical jungles. (As a child, I'd always dreamt of my older self being immersed in tropical jungles. It was time to realise this dream.)

But my new position as a company director was incredibly exhilarating. Many long hours were spent loading up exhibition stands and ordering materials for the buildings. I couldn't tell the difference between a drill bit and a nail gun. I had no idea what anything was. I was in at the deep end and ran around in a state of frenzy. But I was determined, chasing my tail, picking up knowledge as it came. I bought a notebook and scribbled furiously all day long. Everything went into that notebook. Phone numbers. Product details.

Suppliers' names. Their children's names. Everything. It was the only way to retain information and ensure I could refer back to it whenever I felt lost. Which was often.

I was due to fly out to San José in July. But with every passing day, my desire to continue working towards helping this project meant that I was finding it difficult to step away. There were many phone calls I needed to make, the website was being built, and I'd immersed myself in starting work on the business plan for a new product Aidan had designed. I'd found my passion!! It was a start-up! I had to learn, from scratch, how to write a business plan. Aidan was talking about bringing on investors and really going for it. Big time. We needed that business plan! The skills I'd brought with me from my earlier career in both finance and administration all came into play as I started work on creating a process and database which we could use for keeping track of orders. The company was featured in the national press, on the television, in the news, in design journals. The phone was ringing off the hook on most days. The trajectory for the firm looked stratospheric. I had arrived at this business at an incredibly exciting time.

Fate had seemingly brought me to a top-level position, working as Sales Director for this remarkable industrial designer and his incredible eco-buildings firm. Just six months into my work with him, we were contacted by BBC researchers and invited onto *Dragons' Den* to pitch for investment, on BBC TV.

So, I did what any self-respecting soon to be jet-setting 30-year-old would do. I phoned the airline and deferred my flight. The following week, I deferred it once more. After four weeks of dithering and delaying, I eventually left England to catch what was remaining of my long-awaited adventure. I had cut my backpacking adventure down by a month. Why would anyone do this? What did I learn from this? That when you've found a career which challenges and stimulates you and puts you in the driving seat, even a tropical holiday can't compare to the happiness you feel. I was just as happy in the thick of it, at EcoHab, as I would have been on holiday. Therein lies a little pearl of wisdom. 'Create a life for yourself that you wouldn't need to take a holiday from.' I think I'd actually found it. That in itself was quite remarkable.

Just twelve months after I had returned from Costa Rica, the cracks started to show. Customer complaints were coming in. Bills were going unpaid for longer than they should've been. The problem with the business was not the idea or the concept, but the quality of the offering and my lack of experience when it came to running a business. Corners were being cut in manufacturing and the product itself was not as 'eco' as I had initially envisaged.

Our wealthy philanthropist client, Dawn Gibbins, had emailed me personally to directly question my morals and ask why I was still working there and why I wasn't using my skills working for a more ethical firm. Given that I had been working with Aidan on her project for the past twelve months, we had got to know each other and we'd become friends. She liked Aidan and me but the building wasn't constructed as she'd expected and the lengthy delays were causing her distress. We had run over budget and were still lagging behind after eighteen months of disrupted work on site. There seemed no end to the problems. She had a film crew on site for *My Flat pack Home* and she needed a resolution. We needed to extend the contract again, and ask her for more money to complete this structure. It wasn't going well for us.

The *Dragons' Den* episode was due to be aired in mid-September and I was both excited and yet worried that we didn't yet have the capabilities to scale up the operations. Many heated conversations arose between myself and Aidan and I questioned the materials and processes behind the product. I recognised that hardwood doors came from jungles of West Africa and Borneo (oh, the horror!). If only to add to the situation, we had a family of enormous rats who'd decided to make our small joinery workshop their home. We had no running water and a chemical Portaloo served as the main facilities for the team on site. This included me. As much as I loved working on a building site in the early days, it was beginning to take its toll as we headed into a second winter on a cold farm with little heating. Aidan was as ever, optimistic and charming and he reassured me that he was happy with the operations, and insisted that I push ahead with sales, administration and marketing. He wished to retain full control over the fabrication and product design. No, we can't outsource. No, we can't change the design. We looked at moving premises but we didn't yet have the order book to support it. Try as I might, I lacked the experience and the authority to successfully traverse from the current operations to the business I believed it could be.

As a minority shareholder, I didn't have the power to, either. I started to try and control other elements of the business but I started to make mistakes and spoke unkindly to Aidan on several occasions which I regret dreadfully, because it was his business, and he's a great guy. As a director of a business, but not a significant shareholder, you find yourself in a dichotomy. You hold the responsibility of the business performance but lack the power to control it. Therefore it's a difficult role because you shoulder the responsibility for the success of the enterprise and yet you are still very much an employee who needs to take direction from the owner, whether or not they call you a business partner. I started to wonder what my long-term prospects were. I remember asking him once, 'Aidan, if you were manufacturing baked beans, would you prefer to be Heinz, or Tesco's economy range?'

Whereas I aligned myself firmly and resolutely with Heinz and admired the idea of top-end, high-quality, premium branding, Aidan responded with 'Economy' and preferred instead the low-end, high volume model. I knew then that we simply didn't have the same vision for the business and my time had come to an end.

START AGAIN. MULTIPLE TIMES

Success is not final, failure is not fatal:
it is the courage to continue that counts.

Winston S. Churchill

As someone who leans towards symptoms of paralysing depression when it decides to take hold, I felt myself slip into the familiar dark cloud. I left the company quite suddenly when I discovered I was pregnant and that the *Dragons' Den* offer wasn't the solution to our problems. The stress of running the business in the form that it took was reaching crisis point and, to my surprise and that of those around me, I found myself walking away from what I'd initially thought was the job of my dreams to start all over again. It was through this experience that I learnt a lot about the importance of leadership and vision. Aidan was an amazingly charismatic inventor and creative entrepreneur. He was the true leader of this organisation. I needed to respect that. Being with O-Pod wasn't my destiny. It was a job. I was never going to be happy as an employee, even at that level. It was a remarkable experience, but I discovered that I was, in fact, an entrepreneur just like him and I really needed to fly.

But there was something about the O-Pod that was etched into my soul. I was enamoured of the concept of roundhouses and their connection to Stonehenge, pre-neolithic civilisations and the shape of our planet and everything else in it. I had discovered that there were at least three other companies in the world who were building in a similar way. The Americans built roundhouses in the hurricane belt, for they were amazingly aerodynamic and never blew over! I loved how unapologetically radical is the idea of building roundhouses as opposed to square ones. There's something in that which is fantastically rebellious. Through the course of my time with Aidan, I'd spoken to archaeologists and anthropologists, architects and energy-workers. It dawned on me that I had happened upon something quite incredible. Circular buildings are both defiant and hilariously logical. They exist in direct opposition to how modern civilisations perceive normality and yet in complete alignment with the perceived normality of our ancestors and that of other species. 'Birds don't build square nests!!' I'd passionately declare to those around me; sometimes, I talked about it so much, my friends would hide from me at garden parties or family events.

It was a deep and enduring passion. But, the vehicle was entirely wrong.

So, there I was once again, working in a café during the day whilst I threw myself into drawing up a business plan and making scale models at night. Becoming more and more heavily pregnant as the months passed, I was gripped with a burning desire to create something of *value*. Inspired by the shape and the apex roof light of the O-Pod but swapping out many of the materials with ethical, sustainable alternatives, a local supply chain and more rustic Scandinavian log cabin-style aesthetic, I scribbled my ideas out until late at night. I drew scale designs, figuring out how the floor panels might work and what the roof would look like. I researched timber-framing and construction techniques. I learnt about the qualities of different insulation materials. I envisioned a high-quality building which was circular, but radiated the aspirations and the ethos of a holistic healthcare brand or organic food brand. I drew up designs taking inspiration from buildings around the world and identified sections of cartwheels and seashells for aesthetic components like beams and trusses. Being careful to adhere to the golden ratio, I studied books on sacred geometry, the psychology of space, and circular architectural designs spanning the centuries.

None of this changed the fact that I was out of work again. Pregnant and starting from zero. But the powerful motivation of a beautiful idea, a burning desire to bring it into reality and a crystal clear image in my head of what it would look like. The wealthy philanthropist who sent me the email had been the catalyst I needed to recognise that it was time to jump again.

Several weeks after resigning, a local businessman called Geoff who knew Aidan approached me. He loved the *Dragons' Den* episode and he wanted to get involved. If a Dragon wasn't investing, he wanted to invest himself. Geoff was a pharmaceutical chemist and incredible salesman who'd created a really interesting business in the cleaning sector. They manufacture environmentally friendly cleaning products which basically consist of bacteria cultures. The hungry bacteria literally gobble up dirt and germs in the same way that yeast eats sugar. I personally felt that it was the most groundbreaking product on the market and I still maintain that. At the time, he kept himself busy as a distributor of cleaning products from America to exclusive hotels and yacht companies. Geoff liked the idea of the O-Pod eco-buildings. I maintained that I was no longer working on O-Pod and was instead working on my own designs. He loved that idea and suggested that I work from his office and he would fund the construction of a prototype, for shares in the new company.

We called the new enterprise 'Gemstone Eco-Pods' which for the life of me, I can't imagine why.

In my heavily pregnant state, the café owners let me go. I couldn't work in the café any more. I quickly ran out of money. I sold my car to support myself and hoped I could make it until the maternity benefits kicked in. I travelled to the office most days to work on the business plan and try to drum up some business. Geoff brought in a joiner who could help us build a prototype. Finally, after nine long months, my daughter was born, the prototype was complete and we were ready to go! Clutching a two-week-old baby in my arms, I sat in an armchair next to a tall wooden window in a beautiful sun-filled roundhouse. The internal space was better than I'd imagined, with glossy bamboo floors, Farrow and Ball paint finish on the wood-panelled walls and a breathtaking vaulted ceiling which rose above us to the circular skylight in the very apex. It was named Dreamcatcher by Dawn. We were all delightedly chuckling at the incredible achievement we'd made at the launch of our very first Eco-Pod. It looked remarkable, with long, slim wooden windows, a steep-pitched zinc roof and a natural wooden exterior. I was delighted that we'd made it this far. But I had only a few months of maternity allowance left. I was running out of money.

Six months after the initial unveiling of the Gemstone Eco-Pods unit (thankfully the product had now been renamed as The Rotunda), my personal and financial situation was spiralling rapidly downhill. As a new mum with a six-month-old baby, I was heading into the inevitable breakdown of the relationship with her father. The situation was looking decidedly bleak. One cold and blustery January morning I was home alone with my tiny daughter and crying inconsolably down the phone to my hilariously funny and larger than life Dutch friend, Olga. She lived a mile or so away and she and I had been firm friends since working together in the Italian restaurant a few years earlier.

When she'd listened to me snivelling for the best part of fifteen minutes she drew a sharp intake of breath and with the air of abrupt finality, she gave me a simple set of precise instructions. '*Stay there. Pack a bag. I'm coming to get you.*' And in that minute, hung up, drove immediately to my house and swept both me and my baby into her car, into her house and out of that relationship forever.

So, there we were. Practically homeless. A single mum, sleeping on a friend's sofa with a six-month-old baby, at the age of 32. Failed start-up entrepreneur. After more than six months, the new business was still no further ahead. I had now completely run out of money, maxed my credit cards and all I had to my name was nothing more than a sparsely populated website which I'd built myself, and a small 4m-wide prototype (paid for by Geoff) sitting in a car park by an A-road in rural Cheshire. When Esmee was old enough to be bundled into a pram or a car seat, I had continued travelling back and forth, from my home in Manchester, to Geoff's office several days a week. Sometimes I would get a lift with one of Geoff's employees. Sometimes I would borrow a car. But without a track record, it is *practically impossible* to convince someone to part with tens of thousands of pounds, no matter how pretty the prototype is. Without testimonials, a comprehensive brochure or a marketing budget, it's even harder to capture the attention of potential clients. I wrote articles and press releases which appeared in design journals and local newspapers. But the very few enquiries I received were difficult to convert into a real-life client. Potential buyers requested site meetings in faraway places and brochures detailing technical information. Without a car, without a budget, without a brochure and without the cash to support such activities I was totally and utterly stuck in neutral and had absolutely no way of hitting first gear and driving it forwards.

What I did have, however, was the most incredible support from O-Pod's larger-than-life philanthropist client. The late Dr Dawn Gibbins, MBE. Sometimes, in the start-up world, you just happen across the most magnificent human beings. She was one of them.

FIND A MENTOR

It was Dawn who encouraged me to take the leap into entrepreneurship and for this I owe a debt of gratitude which will never be paid.

A few weeks after the cataclysmic break-up of Esmee's family life, I finally moved out of Olga's house and packed up the fold-out sofa for the last time. Finally, after weeks of searching, I found a tiny cottage in a little rural village in Cheshire. At the time of finding the rental house, I had no money for the deposit and no way of securing it. I owe a lot to my friend Avril, who I'd known since I was 20. We were inseparable for many years. The fun I had during the decade of my twenties, I owe largely to her. She was a helpful and caring friend. I was standing on the doorstep of her house, one gloomy, desolate morning in February as she passed a cheque for £500 through the door and into my hand. 'Good luck,' she cried, as she blew me a kiss and sent me off on my way. How I would've managed to get a deposit together without help from a friend like this, I have no idea.

With little else but a rucksack of clothes I found myself in an empty cottage in the desolate depths of winter with little to show for my life so far but with a heart bursting full of hope. One morning, I carefully laid out the grocery vouchers which I'd received from the benefits office, alongside the remaining cash I had found in my purse. I spread it out on the old pine table and calculated that I had £23.04 to spend that week. In this situation, every penny literally counts. But, I was strangely happy. Despite what you might be thinking about the reality of this situation, I wasn't in a total quagmire of despair and depression (these moments came in sudden and sporadic bursts but were surprisingly infrequent). I felt positive because I had something to aim for. I had a working laptop and a business plan which I'd worked on since the departure from EcoHab and O-Pod. I was no longer sleeping on a friend's sofa. Things could only get better from this point onwards. The fact that I was sleeping on the floor on a mattress because I couldn't afford a bed was of mere insignificance. Things were going to get better.

Esmee's grandmother, (her dad's mum) a cheerful, vivacious and engaging woman called Yvonne, came to my rescue in those early days. She would drive the 150 mile round trip, almost two hours each way, from Lytham St Annes to my home each and every Monday. I would be free to go and build my business whilst she would take Esmee out for the day. It had now been six months since the prototype was completed and Geoff was starting to question whether I would ever get this thing off the ground. He would come and collect me from the house, or lend me one of his cars so I could travel to him.

I tried everything possible. Writing blogs. Reaching out to garden centres with leaflets. Approaching garden designers and landscape architects. I pointed everyone I could to the direction of my website with enthusiasm and confidence. The way I saw it, I simply had to get this started or I would be stuck for evermore without the means to support my daughter. But still, the sales didn't come.

It was one day in early spring that Geoff left me in the care of one of his employees. This chap had decided that he would train me in the process of selling their vacuum cleaners and cleaning products. After spending a few hours dispassionately designing logos and straplines for bacterial cleaning products, and learning the workings of vacuum cleaners, I finally felt irrationally angry. A fireball of resentment was building in my chest. I was not here to sell vacuum cleaners, I wasn't on the payroll, I wasn't leaving my baby at home with her father to travel out here and sell .... vacuum cleaners!!!

But it was clear that I was failing. I couldn't make it work. Was this my fate? It wasn't long before I ran out of patience and decided not to go back. I couldn't face going to those offices and meeting yet more failure, a consistent brick wall and the seemingly insurmountable task of generating interest for a product which hadn't even hit the market and probably never would. When I got home, I lay in bed and cried and cried for what felt like hours. I cried for the loss of my family, the mess of my entire situation and the loss of my dream. I was alone. I had nothing. I was a useless and delusional person who just wanted, more than anything, for life to go back to normal.

Of course, this situation couldn't be kept under wraps and I had to finally tell Dawn. I called her and poured my heart out following the most recent disaster.

'I can't make it work Dawn,' I cried. 'It's over.' I lay on my mattress on the floor bed and felt totally defeated as I clamped the phone to my ear and awaited her advice, or sympathy.

Dawn is the most cheerful, positive and supportive person you're ever likely to meet. She is also an astonishingly good entrepreneur; her background involved the creation of an international flooring business which she grew to a staggering £45m annual turnover before selling it to an American firm for £35 million. In 2003 she was awarded the Veuve Clicquot Businesswoman of the Year; this places her firmly alongside the ranks of other elusive industry unicorns such as Anita Roddick and Zaha Hadid. Dawn was featured in a 2009 episode of *The Secret Millionaire* Channel 4 TV series, donating £250,000 to three Bristol-based charities. Let's just say, she's a legend. She was my rock in those early days.

'Gemma,' she said. 'It's not over. So what? You fell out with Geoff? You need to rethink this. You just need a factory and a phone line; for when your first order comes in, you know? You will get your business off the ground. I believe in you.' And with that, she told

me that I could set up in her factory. Dawn had a commercial building about eight miles from my home. It was being used to store furniture and accommodate a homeless charity she was helping. OK, so, I'd need to share. But I didn't have my prototype. Geoff had that. I'd agreed to let him keep it so he could turn it into a retail unit.

So, I transitioned again. To another factory, in a rural location in the back end of absolutely nowhere. Esmee was still only tiny, at nine months old. I didn't have a car so I took the bus. Three days a week I'd bundle Esmee up into her pram and trot down the road to catch the no.10 bus into Macclesfield. A short hop across town and I could catch the next bus which trundled along country roads for another twenty minutes to a place called Bosley. The factory was incredibly remote but, a large sweeping tarmac car park gave way to an impressive towering structure of glass and powder-coated steel which set a fantastic tone for the next stage of Rotunda. There was a sealed, dry and immaculately clean warehouse and an enormous open-plan office with floor to ceiling windows and plush, curved sofas which faced jaw-dropping views of the Peak District. One could watch the weather systems roll in over the hills for hours in this magnificent place. On the days I couldn't face the journey, I'd set up a professional telephone number which was redirected to the landline of my tiny cottage.

Dawn was the maternal figure who remained steadfast in her belief that one day my ideas would become successful. She took me under her brightly coloured wing and lent me space to work from in her factory and office, near her hometown in Congleton, Cheshire. As a successful entrepreneur herself, she encouraged and guided me to do my absolute best and further supported me later on by purchasing one of my first ever prototypes for her garden. A legendary character. So, in the very early days, I was travelling to and from an office that was two very long bus journeys from home, with no income and no money to actually take the start-up into any sort of trading position. I persisted around childcare by day, and at night and over the weekends busied myself writing blogs, advertising on free online directories and placing free ads on message boards and outside post offices.

I attended free networking events and spread the word of my fledgling business far and wide through friends and family. Miraculously, a few email enquiries came dribbling in, following on from a publication in a design magazine which had featured the new business and a hand-drawn illustration of the product but still, nothing came to a tangible sale. It's almost impossible, if not downright stupid, to launch a new product into the UK marketplace with no track record, no money to market it and no portfolio of clients. I was beginning to travel into the factory less and worked from my kitchen table a little more. After several months, I knew deep down that I was just spinning my wheels and all of this work may likely come to nothing, but I was already in too deep. I had to push on. At this point, someone actually said to me, 'I don't know why you are pursuing this ridiculous campaign; why don't you just enjoy being a mum and drop it?' But I couldn't face a future which was more uncertain than the one I was already in. If I was deluded, then this was indeed a total waste of time, but at least I was aiming for *something*.

I would sit at the kitchen table, drawing up new designs for the website, or I'd be at my laptop, furiously tapping out long wordy blogs on the tired and battered keyboard until late at night. All in the hope of catching traffic on Google or to capture the interest of someone who might stumble across the website by chance. I applied for grants and wrote long investment proposals to anyone who might be able to support me. Nobody in their right mind would invest in a single mum with zero sales! No matter how much Dawn championed me. I wanted to give up.

I was at home one Thursday in early July when the miraculous happened. My mother had come to visit. We were sat eating lunch, squeezed around the table in my tiny cottage and I was trying desperately to remain cheerful and conversational. Just as I was spearing a little salad potato onto my fork and making crazy faces at my eleven-month-old daughter bouncing around in her high chair, the land line rang in the living room.

I answered, ever hopeful, with a 'Good afternoon, Rotundaaaa-ah, how may I help?' whilst secretly clasping my hands in prayer, as one might imagine in a painfully desperate scene from *Fawlty Towers*. 'Ah. Hello, I am enquiring after one of your garden buildings...' A crackly female voice rippled out from the receiver. I was momentarily paralysed. The voice continued, 'I have seen your website and I am wondering how much a small garden room costs?'

BINGO!

I hurriedly retrieved a pen and started furiously writing down the details of the woman on the other end of the phone. 'Uh-huh, yes, hmmm ... garden room you say, yes, well, I do have a price list I can email across to you; where are you?' The conversation started flowing and before I knew it, I'd made an appointment to visit her at home the following Monday. Ten days later, I had a deposit transferred into the business bank account for the sum of £6,000.

That night I spent lying awake, unable to sleep, in a state of terror and contemplating whether or not I should give the client her money back. The pressure was immense. 'This is a ridiculous idea. Who *am I* to be constructing buildings? I'm not even a builder! What madness is this?!?' I would scold myself as I lay in bed staring into the darkness. I heard Esmee cry in the next room. I went to soothe her and settled her back to sleep. When I clambered back into bed I felt sick and uneasy. I was right to be worried. I hadn't the foggiest idea how to build it. I just had a stack of drawings and some architectural plans but I'd not actually built one *for real.* I had been trying to make a sale for almost two years and now I had one I didn't want the responsibility of fulfilling it! That was, in many ways, the scariest moment of the start-up journey.

I held a crisis meeting with Dawn the following morning. 'What if I can't build it?' I cried. 'What will I do?' Dawn chose to ignore my excruciatingly pessimistic monologue and instead presented me with a cheque for £5,000. 'Here's a loan, Gemma,' she said as she pressed it into my hand. 'For cash flow.' Smiling at me as if it were the easiest thing in the world. I pulled myself together and phoned a joiner who I knew from an earlier enterprise. He was out of work. I had my first sub-contractor.

I was suddenly, and amazingly ... in business.

As a hesitant or yet-to-be entrepreneur, you may be of the opinion that the most terrifying element of starting your own business is quitting your job. I agree with you. It most definitely is. But what nobody had warned me about is the fear which arises from securing your first contract and employing your first member of staff. This is where you really feel fear on a whole new level. All of the self-doubt and pessimism that exists within your subconscious mind will rise up to paralyse you once again. You actually have to DO what you have been promising people you *could do*. And there is nobody to hold your hand. No employer to be accountable to, or to support and train you as you learn a new trade. What if you mess it up? Unless you are experienced in this industry and a highly capable individual, the likelihood is that you will fall flat on your face in the early days. This is where you need to run the gauntlet. Cross the chasm between 'idealism' and 'realism'. Is this business really going to become what you'd imagined it to be? Do you have the skills, ideas, knowledge and effectiveness to actually deliver? Could you face losing a client's trust? Their money? Could you handle a staff dispute, or manage the accounting and tax returns? How could you face it if your best member of staff resigns or if the market takes a nose dive? What will you need to really make it as an entrepreneur?

You need to be *brave*. Step forward regardless of the fear and the lack of knowledge, experience and financial support that would make this transition more bearable. You have to accept that you are learning and that your business is brand new. You are one of the pioneers – starting from scratch. The acceptance of the fact that you need to start somewhere, even it if means pain and hard work for little or no money for the first couple of years is actually an incredible adventure. Bravery doesn't mean stupidity – it means, proceeding forwards despite the fact that you are out on your own with little support. But if you *believe* that you have something of value, others will too.

Eventually.

Tips I can give you, which I have learnt from my mistakes are:

- Do not fail to appreciate the importance of having some money for generating sales and investing in marketing. I did it with no money – this was a huge mistake. Had I the time to do it again, I would have set aside/leveraged/borrowed funds from the first investor, to use as a marketing budget and saved myself the painful eighteen months of trudging into work trying to make sales with no money to advertise my product.

- Be careful who you partner with. For both of your sakes. It might seem like a match made in heaven when a friendly business person offers to bankroll your idea but you must be clear what your roles are and what would happen if the project fails to launch after a certain period of time.

- Learn as much as you can about the marketplace and the key players within it. How are they marketing themselves? What is their story? Why are they in demand? What else is happening in industry at the moment which complements your idea?

- If there is one skill which is absolutely *vital* to the success of your start-up it is: *learn to become a salesperson...*

BECOME A SALESPERSON

Opportunities don't happen. You create them.

Chris Grosser

Senior Sales Consultant at Tesla

When you think of sales, you might be inclined to shudder at the prospect of door-to-door salesmen or aggressive salespeople with terrifyingly manipulative deal-closing techniques. But, my dear, hesitant, soon-to-be entrepreneur, you may be surprised to learn that sales are driven by good customer service, great communication, the sharing of stories, ethics, a willingness to help, to solve problems, and most of all, active listening. Your sales are the energy and the fuel which runs through your fledgling organisation as your lifeblood. Sales require skills in healthy, engaging and authentic communication, which comes as much from listening as it does from speaking.

Sales and Marketing usually get bundled up into one department in many businesses which I find baffling for they are poles apart in terms of their approach and execution. Marketing is communicating a broad message. Your brand, your ethos, your story. It literally reaches out and connects with people who share the same view of the world as you do. Marketing is visual, it's ethereal, it's a witty motto or an inspiring emblem. The signature and the calling card of your identity and brand. Imagine putting your product on a billboard emblazoned with a snappy strapline to capture the attention of your target market. Everyone can see the sleek product and a strapline. That's you. It captures the attention of your audience. Marketing works through social media campaigns run as competitions or give-aways. Marketing is the 'big picture' message. Core Values. Your problem solving capabilities. The marketing doesn't by itself close the sales. It opens the door and breaches the awareness of the consumer. I see marketing as a route to cultivate brand awareness and show the world that you exist. Once a marketing message has been recognised several times (the rule of seven says that the prospective buyer should hear or see the marketing message at least seven times before they buy from you) a customer may contact you for further information.

This is where Sales comes in. It's a genuine human connection between you and your prospective client. The first conversation is usually the start of a trusting relationship and exchange of ideas and the outline of costs and benefits. Whereas sales is predominantly understood as a transaction between a buyer and a seller, the sales skill is simply being able to communicate positively, enthusiastically and negotiate well with another person. Often, I've found, sales come not from giving a price but from listening intently, finding a common ground and finding a shared interest, making conversation and simply being in the position to be able to say 'yes' to their request for help. Most often, the prospective client is reaching out to you with an idea of what they want. They are just waiting for you to say 'yes'. That's all.

The four fundamental skills pertaining to salespeople are:

Confidence – maintaining a positive attitude.
Resilience – communicating with conviction.
Active listening – understanding the customers' needs.
Rapport building – selling your personality.

Most of all, I have discovered that it comes down to a belief system. You *believe* in your product or idea so much that you can easily convince others to believe in it too. By having such belief in what you are doing, you are communicating a message to others that the world *can be a better place*. You are communicating authentically. If you are selling something you don't believe in, you will be caught out. Everyone can sense a fake sales person who is pushing something they really don't care about. Your job is to be the storyteller, the voice of reassurance, the friendly voice on the end of the phone to bounce ideas around with. You can illustrate how you can help your client and paint a picture in their mind of how your service will improve their lives and eliminate their problem. This isn't just beneficial to potential customers, but can be hugely crucial to retaining key employees, raising capital and starting a movement.

Sales skills will enable you to hire the best people, bring on an investor or work with other organisations (such as, partnering with distributors, competitors or setting up a franchise). When you are a small start-up, you could find yourself in a position where you're bootstrapping and you have little funds to splash around on big salaries. So, how do you hire great people who may get a better salary elsewhere? You sell them the vision and the ethics of the company. Your company is set for the stars! You believe so much that your company is better, has better chances of success, will live on to flourish and become a market leader, has the capacity to solve problems that your competitors cannot. You can *sell this* to your future employees. Besides, it's not always the extra money which entices people into a new job.

A recent UK & Global Job Satisfaction Survey undertaken in 2021 discovered that:

> 72% of millennials class 'having a job with meaning' as the most important factor in their work – *Does your start-up have meaning?*
>
> Only 3 in 10 millennials say that salary is the most important factor when choosing to accept a job offer – *What else can you offer?*

> Over half of millennials have left a job because they felt the employer's values did not align with their own – *What are your values and are you communicating them?*
>
> 64% of British workers would rather have a low-paid job they love, than a high-paid job which they do not enjoy – *What can you give an employee to ensure they love their job?*

This most likely speaks to you anyway, soon-to-be entrepreneur. You are probably considering leaving your profession for reasons other than the size of your salary. When you are designing your business, you must be absolutely convinced of nothing other than your vision. You must be so certain of success that you are able to easily communicate this to everyone else. Even if it bores them to tears. If you aren't passionate about your idea, how will you hope to sell it to others?

Being able to sell will enable you to drive your business forwards. If you can't sell, don't have the attributes to become a sales person for your brand or simply don't want to sell, you must recognise this and hire or partner with those who can. You *can* be an introvert and set up a business. If you are, for example, a scientist or an engineer who has designed a ground-breaking new technology or appliance but you simply don't want to deal with sales, I would recommend partnering with an outgoing and charismatic partner who can do the front-of-house work so you can work in blissful solitude in your studio or workshop and focus on what you excel at. The company roles can be split into 'sales' and 'technical' – you should both be very clear on your roles and work alongside each other to build the business this way.

So, rather than learning to become a salesperson, proving your concept to a new business partner who can be 'sales' should be your first port of call. Design your product, get the prototype constructed – and present it, not to your client base or the UK market but to a business partner who can manage this side of the business for you. If you believe in the company, you can hire others who can cascade this down to your clients through their communication. Hire excellent communicators to help!

Steve Jobs believed in his company so much that he recognised he had the power to change the world with his technology. Rather than feel like he's crazy for having such grand ideas, he vocalised his belief to hire his CEO, the Pepsi executive, John Sculley. When trying to lure him to the company, he asked, 'Do you want to sell sugar water for the rest of your life, or do you want to come with me and change the world?' Well, how's that for an invitation? Changing the world.

Isn't that what we all wish to do? Why exactly do you want to start a business? Just to pay the mortgage and exist......? Or do you sincerely believe that you can create something of value? If you venture out into the world with your bold and courageous idea, I am betting that you will change the course of other people's lives. By sending your idea out into the world, you may even change thousands or millions of lives. When you ponder on whether you have any sales ability, tap into that internal force which is guiding you to establish your business. What is it for? Why are you so keen to start it? Who will it impact?

A client of mine has a beautiful social enterprise called Riverside House. It has been created to serve two distinct needs. One, is to regenerate an old patch of derelict, neglected wasteland which sits by a canal in an urban location in the Black Country of England. The other, is to provide education and engagement for people of all ages with learning difficulties and issues with mental health. On meeting him, I was immediately impressed by his passion for the project. It was so genuine and so instantly likeable. With a warm, beaming smile and an infectious laugh, he welcomed me into the site to show me the raised vegetable beds, the wildlife pond, and the oak-framed willow-weaving workshop and blacksmithing area. Recently hailed as a 'groundbreaking social regeneration project', Lloyd has developed it slowly, over the course of several years. Now he has an established business, a fantastic career for himself and his employees and the type of job satisfaction many of us could only dream of. What was once an area of derelict scrubland is now a stunning ecologically sound Health & Wellbeing Centre. Lloyd believes that, 'Meaningful, social activities can make a significant difference to the quality of our lives. This is achieved through the practice of traditional crafts, arts, ecology, heritage, and food and nutrition.' What is so unbelievable about this project? That Lloyd was made redundant several times by his previous employer. He was not sitting on fortunes neither did he have other businesses to support him but he had a fantastic idea which solved a lot of problems for many people. After securing the site for just £1 from the Local Authority he went forward with his vision and secured grants and support for his radical idea. At the time of writing this, he now has 18 students enrolled on his courses and he is building two additional classrooms and a café. Propelled forward with a clear and unwavering vision of his contribution to the world, he can easily communicate his ideas to others, for the passion is undeniable. When you have a vision, and you can see how this can benefit others, the passion, and the sales, will flow naturally.

Lloyd chuckles as he tells me, 'I'm no sales person. I've tried to sell things before but I was terrible at it. But with this project, it's easy to communicate and sell it to others. Because I feel so passionate about the project and I have so much love for it, it just flows. In the past I used to be afraid of public speaking but now I'm not fazed by any of it.'

Now, I'll give you one tip for sales. I've learnt that the best way to sell is to find something you believe in. Something that inspires you and fires you up. Something you get passionate about.

You will not need to 'learn' to become a salesperson. You will naturally talk to people in an enthusiastic and passionate way. For it's your belief that sells.

Are you getting it yet? What do you care about? What do you believe about it? Why do you care about it so much? How can you communicate this? You'll sell ice to the Eskimos, my dear female entrepreneur.

WHERE TO BEGIN

Your time is limited, so don't
waste it living someone else's life.

Steve Jobs

This book is in your hands because deep down you recognise that this is simply your brain resisting change and you *can and must* push through it despite your negative thought patterns.

It's natural for a first-time entrepreneur to wonder whether this is total delusion. You are actually going through the natural process of assessing risk. The human brain always looks for problems. This is what Seth Godin, a leadership coach and author calls the Lizard Brain or what Steven Pressfield, an American author, describes as 'the resistance'. This is the voice in our head telling us to slow down, to compromise, that we can't or won't be enough, and that we're punching above our weight.

One thing I've learnt over my career so far is that even the most successful people feel the same amount of fear as the rest of us. They have learnt to push through it. Can you switch off your lizard brain and jump?

Imagine someone about to jump off a comfortable cruise ship into the deep, dark ocean below. What the frustrated cruise-jumper doesn't yet know, is that a dinghy is awaiting him below. That dinghy is his to steer and will carry him to a tropical island of jungles and mountains where he will live the life of his dreams, packed with adventure and fulfilment. What's more, along the way he'll encounter a great number of other dinghies, all whizzing along in different directions, driven by people grinning insanely, just like him! He'll forge lifelong friendships with like-minded people who assist and join him on his journey. He no longer needs to try to fit in with the cruise-goers; they were never his tribe.

But if he doesn't jump he'll never know ... his thoughts are a whirr ... he's been stuck on this cruise ship for weeks, months even. Everyone else seems quite happy and is enjoying themselves so then why can't he? His spirit is restless, he craves adventure, but is terrified to leave the safety and convenience of the ship. But it's just so pointless to live for enjoyment alone without seeking a life of purpose and adventure. He pauses and gazes at the water below while wondering, 'What's wrong with me?' Feeling quite agitated and annoyed with himself now, he's wishing he could be more like the others. Little does he know, it's not HIM that's the problem. He's a true spirit. It's his authentic self calling him. For deep inside, he knows that there is something greater awaiting him. Crazy huh? But, will he jump? Will YOU?

I was a latecomer to the entrepreneurial realm. I believe it is due to the fact that I was always the child who didn't quite fit a 'winner' personality type. Typical of a lot of entrepreneurs, I disliked school and did little to further myself academically. The middle child of five siblings, I was the forgetful one, the clumsy one, the creative one, the dreamer. While my parents were proudly sending older siblings off to university to study sciences or engineering, my future was handled with quizzical ambivalence. University was not presented to me as an option. I was never meant to be an achiever, at least that's what society taught me from an early age. If I asked about university, my parents quickly changed the subject. The future for me was likely that of a housewife. At best, I was told to look at becoming a veterinary nurse. Apparently I lacked the intellect to be a vet. My sister became a vet. She was a Grade A student at everything. I resented her for it. I grew up believing that my objective in life was to find a man who had a decent career so I could be a housewife like my mother and hers before her. This was all my mother suggested I'd likely succeed at.

Unfortunately, we all suffer from the same entrenched belief system that we are not good enough. This is true for most of us at least. The alarming consequence of this is, of course, that a huge percentage of people who are indeed capable of making wonderful and positive changes to our society are yet to step into the arena for fear of failure. Should they (this includes you, by the way) realise their potential, step out of their comfort zones, own their lives and become entrepreneurs they could enrich thousands or millions of lives with their ideas. We might've solved a great number of problems by now but this huge wealth of untapped talent languishes under a sorrowful pile of self-doubt. This leaves us, as a society, at a disadvantage. For there are many sociopaths, narcissists and psychopaths who will gladly climb the ladder of success, monopolise markets, and build wildly successful empires in the name of profit. They will continue to do so because they are not challenged by the everyday man and woman like you or me.

If you listen to the 'resistance' you will never find the courage to begin. Be bold, be brave, be firm in your resolve. If it's failure you're concerned about, then it's a good idea to start a business immediately, for you will discover that through failure your capacity for learning and growth can thrive. I cannot reassure you that you won't fail. You might. Not all of your business ideas will take off. But a sapling doesn't fail to take root and grow because it's worried that the sun won't shine. It grows onwards and upwards, twisting and turning along the way, pushing aside rocks and paving slabs, reaching towards the sun. You are the sapling. It's your job to establish your root system and drive your spirit and ambitions upwards and outwards despite the obstacles, despite the naysayers (for there will be many) and despite your subconscious mind sabotaging your opportunity for success.

That's not to say you shouldn't be mindful of the dangers that lurk ahead. Understanding that it won't be easy should never be a reason to abandon your ideas. Appreciating that it's not a gentle meander along a riverbank but a dramatic climb up an inhospitable mountain terrain fraught with danger. This, my friend, is exactly what we're signing up for. The challenge! I commenced my start-up journey feeling remarkably ambitious. What I had believed to be a meandering, uninterrupted path (to what would surely culminate in guaranteed success), suddenly ascended up to a rough terrain with huge embankments to scale followed by a couple of equally steep and cataclysmic falls. The trail, although enlightening in the way that no other career could possibly offer, flung me into a closely avoided bankruptcy, grief, persistent self-doubt, my first £million revenues, financial success, incredible friendships, deceit, fraud, sabotage, and most recently, the theft and loss of an entire organisation, coordinated by those I trusted the most.

Most of the mistakes I made as a start-up founder are primarily down to the fact that I consistently lacked the self-confidence to speak up when I should have; that I allowed others to take too much control; and that I avoided conflict with dominating personality types. Coupled with the fact that I took the difficult route, in a difficult male-dominated industry with little experience in the field in which I chose to work, I neglected to run background checks on the staff and investors I brought into my organisation. My greatest mistakes were the very best lessons. Lessons in entrepreneurship, most definitely. Lessons in psychology and people, yes. But, the most important lessons are the ones whereby we learn deep truths about ourselves and our character. Where our blind spots are. Where we fall short and let ourselves and others down. What we need to do to become better leaders. Learning is a continual journey. If you want to learn as much as you can, then there is very little time to delay; you must get off the starting blocks. If you're committed to a career path which is so unbelievably bonkers yet so ridiculously thrilling, you'll soon understand what it can bring on a personal and societal level. Especially if you're an activist. Thrill seekers, this is your moment. Grasp your life firmly by the hands and direct your energy into accessing freedom for you and for a multitude of others.

So, once you have stumbled across your first idea, what should you do?

One small word I'll give you is this: Act.

It kept me motivated throughout the difficult and time-consuming early start-up phase of my first business and I just knew that if I did nothing else, I needed to act.

This life is an act. The world's a stage. Your stage. You're an actor within the great play of life. It's up to you whether you write your own script and act in a way which is authentic and true to yourself or whether you play someone's sidekick role instead. Even worse, you may end up sitting on the sidelines watching, as a passive member of the audience. Once your idea has revealed itself to you, you need to identify whether it's got the potential to go the distance.

ACT NOW. Do something small to set the wheels in motion. Set up a notes folder. Draw a mind map of all of the things you love to do. Problems which concern you. Products which you could improve. A new type of venture which you could imagine being a customer of, if it existed. Think up company names/product names. Put yourself in the seat of someone buying this product or service – how would it make them feel? Buy a notebook specifically for your new business. Look at purchasing a website domain. Just one small act can be the foundation for the next stage.

Act on your impulse. Don't overstretch yourself and try to do too much all at once. Designing a business is an organic process, it will take time, more time than perhaps you've envisaged. So don't rush it. But do start building small pieces at a time. What you might find is, if you don't act impulsively and quickly, the idea quickly dissipates and the negative thought chatter takes over.

When you have your idea in mind and you've brought it into reality in some small way, the real research can begin:

Is it in alignment with current trends and present-day thinking?

Do you have a realistic solution for a big enough market?

Is anyone else already doing this? If not, is there a good reason why/have they failed?

Can you provide one sentence about a typical customer and another about what you're offering them?

What products do they currently buy?

What are they looking for?

Where will your business be based? Online? Shop? Location?

How do you envisage the business looking in 3, 5 and 10 years time?

Unfortunately 60% of new UK businesses fail within 3 years and 20% of those within just 12 months. A large percentage of start-ups fail because of a lack of market demand. Getting the foundation right is essential to future success. The point of your start-up is not to make money. It's not to be famous. It's to solve a meaningful problem for other people. If you do your research, you might just find that there is market demand for your idea, saving you the heartache that the other 60% are unfortunately going to suffer.

Ultimately, people pay for a problem to be removed. You fix their tap, you deliver their vegetables, you repair their car, you do their administrative work. You get paid. Your business is to discover what you can do to help others and go out there and communicate this to them.

'But I don't know enough about this industry!!' Here we go. Did you hear that? Your lizard brain is back, trying to squeeze your expansive mind back into its box again. Cast aside the annoying whisper of the lizard brain and consider this for a moment. As an entrepreneur you are an architect of ideas and a facilitator of new concepts. You are not limited by industry, sector or experience. Your profession spans industries. You do not need a university degree to have a good idea. In fact, there is no other profession on earth that allows you to step in and out of any industry that takes your fancy. A serial entrepreneur may start out in technology and then sidestep into the luxury hotel market. Provided you have an idea that can benefit that industry and a willingness to learn and connect with others who can assist you along the way, anything is possible.

Please remember, it is not your job to know everything. This is where your key members of staff and advisors come in, once you've got it off the ground. All you need is an idea with genuine value or a problem that needs solving, an idea as to how you might go about solving it/creating it, and then you're ready to go! The details are then worked out with your employees and subcontractors. For example, if you have an idea for a new piece of hardware, seek the services of a hardware engineer or an electrical engineer. Put your idea forward and ask them to design it with you. You might find that it's wise to team up with this key person for the long haul and offer them shares in your company or split your company 50/50 with them. All you need is the VISION.

There are plenty of architects, engineers, designers, chefs, ecologists, scientists, textile manufacturers and skilled technicians in the country whose job it is to know the details. You are the vision and the coordinator and the driver.

When I first started out, I fell into the trap of beating myself up because I didn't know the finer technical details of my industry as well as most time-served joiners or tradesmen. The pressure I'd put myself under before entering a client meeting was immense. I'd crumble if a client asked me about the technical aspects of installing a mains electrical supply or the required fall of pipework for plumbing underneath a building. What I was forgetting was that although a sound understanding of the industry and product is of course necessary, the details were for the technicians. Nowadays, if any of those questions arise I smile and advise them that I'll refer back to the structural engineer/plumber/architect or electrician. I am the designer of the concept and the builder of the brand and the business, not necessarily a skilled plumber, builder or engineer. And thank god for that. For it is being an entrepreneur that makes a company thrive. Remember, you are the pilot. It is essential that you know your aircraft and that you can chart your flight path, coordinate with ground staff and manage your crew effectively. It is not your responsibility to construct the aircraft from scratch, nor should you concern yourself with cooking the in-flight meals, creating new flight paths or designing an airport terminal. You must develop your skills in leadership and communication. You are there to provide your team with work and drive your vision forward. That is all you need focus on.

WHAT ARE YOUR VALUES? WHERE DOES VALUE LIE?

We can't solve problems by using the same kind of thinking we used when we created them.

Albert Einstein

attributed

Before you've even designed your first prototype or set about with your brand or website, it's worth pondering the value of your product or service. I mean this in a literal sense. You see, you set out on a crusade to start a business and you could have in your mind a concept of a product which you are really keen to test in the marketplace. This product could be a sure thing as far as you are concerned and you're all fired up and ready to go. But STOP! Don't go a step further. Before you set out on your journey, take some time to think about where the *value* lies.

For this is where the strength of your brand lies and sets the tone of your company culture.

What are the values you are proposing with your venture? What is the story behind your brand? Can you visualise the entire life cycle? This product will not only affect your lifestyle and wellbeing but that of everyone it will touch. The quality of both your design and your business mindset (ethos, culture and values) will affect the success rate and the happiness factor of your business and everyone in it. The lasting effects of your early decision-making will live on in our society for decades or even several generations after you've made them. Please remember that everything you put out into the world will have an impact on the lives of many other people, habitats and wildlife. Do you realise that you will be touching the lives of millions, or even billions of people either directly or indirectly through your start-up? If you ignore your conscience to make money while distracting yourself from the negative impact that you might have on another person or country, this could prove a difficult enterprise, for you and the whole of our society long term.

A well-polished piece of hardwood timber from West Africa would look incredible as a handle to your new bread knife range, but there is likely to be a swathe of rainforest which lies razed to the ground and an indigenous tribe struggling to make ends meet. You may not see them or feel them directly but your choice as an innovator and business owner will affect them. Your business may grow rapidly and the supply for your product may be directly responsible for the destruction of a habitat that others need for their survival. A phrase I live by is, 'If you always do what you've always done, you'll always get what you've always got' (Henry Ford). You, the innovator are a creator. You are bringing a fresh idea to the world. You have value. Your values will live on through your enterprise. You will inspire others by taking bold action.

Unfortunately it's not always *what we buy* that dictates the state of the environment and our wellbeing. It's what our retailers or supermarkets buy (to sell to us) from the innovators and manufacturers that is the real problem. The guilt that is placed on the shoulders of innocent consumers is wholly unjust. All too often we are told that we can't eat fish because the ocean is dying and the ghost nets are killing marine life. Buying tuna is killing dolphins. That we can't buy anything wrapped in or made of plastic because it's choking our seas. That carrier bags are being swallowed by whales. Slug pellets are poisoning the hedgehogs in our gardens. Rat poison is killing the owls and birds of prey that eat the rodents. And so on it goes. The damage we do to ourselves and the wider environment with the products we use is overwhelming. We therefore scrutinise packaging and labels for the ingredients in our food which might be damaging the rainforests in Borneo. We dutifully bring our reusable jute bags to the shops for fear of taking a plastic carrier bag home. We check for a certificate on our garden furniture to ascertain that the timber is sustainable. We lie awake at night worrying about the state of the planet and vow to shop at our local 'plastic free shop' from now on and banish our children's Barbie dolls to make ourselves feel better.

'Woah there! Hang on a minute!!' I cry, in disbelief at the utter ridiculousness of this entire situation. **'Why is this stuff even on the shelves??!'** Who enabled this to happen? Why must we, the busy mum, the caring grandparent or the ambitious young student, be spending hours of our life agonising over the products in our supermarket trolley when we simply trust that the manufacturers are doing their jobs correctly and not destroying the planet with unethical practice? Why is this OUR fault? We are the consumer. It isn't our job to be investigating the ethical code of practice of every manufacturer we buy from. We trust that those in charge have an ethical conscience. We buy what's put in front of us. It's there for us, sitting under a promotional banner in our local supermarket or flashing up on our television screens in an alluring advert. Why are we being encouraged to buy products that are toxic to us and harming the planet? Who did this?? Who's to blame here?!

You would tie yourself in knots and refuse to buy anything at all if you were to investigate the true nature of everything you bought. Many people are now refusing to play the game of consumerism and have changed their lives to accommodate this value system. Minimalism is a wonderful way to reduce the impact, as a consumer. But, as a *creator*, your job is to create something and sell it. Grow it, evolve, and create a secure financial lifestyle for yourself. If you are about to become a creator, you must create something long-lasting which will sustain the needs of the world we are swiftly moving towards, not the world of yesterday's ambivalence. In this era, we have to think about how the world is evolving. We need to accept that it's now time to consider and improve upon the mistakes the industry has made. To create something new, right now, without addressing the urgency of making recompense and creating something infinitely better, would be business suicide.

Unfortunately too many big businesses have shelved ethical practices for the sake of shareholder profits. They do not feel the slightest bit guilty and will happily pass the guilt to you, innocent, trusting consumer that you are. They remain hopeful that you will not notice. They will sell you the cheapest product possible at the highest possible price and will be laughing at your expense while fine dining at their elaborate shareholders' meetings and quaffing back the champagne. The ruthless business owner will take natural and precious resources and sell them to you without ever putting anything back. Those of us who care about our planet see this as blatant theft. The actions taken by big businesses and corporations are nothing short of criminal. This is the depressing reality we all live with. It will not change unless you and I create alternatives and direct consumers elsewhere, sparing them remorse and instead giving them peace of mind. Small start-ups do not take customers nor their resources for granted. We appreciate them. The dinosaurs of industry will eventually die out. The future of business lies with normal, rational and caring people who feel emotion, who possess humility and create a business around genuinely serving their customers, employees and the wider world. The higher value proposition will always rise to the top. Presently, there aren't enough competitors in the game – *we need you* in it!

You see, it would make both you and your future employees so much happier if you could trade without burdening your customers with guilt and suspicion. They can happily buy from you without the need to scrutinise your product labels or feel guilty about your supply chain. This will come back to you threefold. You will gain trust and credibility (your brand will be strong and memorable, great for word of mouth marketing thus reducing your advertising budget), you will gain more traction with sales which creates more revenue for you (growth and prosperity!), and you will have content and enthusiastic employees who share your vision and know they are part of something inspirational. Happy employees means more productivity and a better company culture; you keep your best people because they won't want to leave you.

Imagine this. Two manufacturing firms in England. Both create plastic toys for children. One manufacturer in Cardiff decides to make Christmas stocking gifts, little toy soldiers that are inexpensive to produce and derive maximum profit for the shareholders. A huge production line is endlessly churning out millions of little moulded plastic shapes that, once assembled, make a basic solider with no discernible features but with movable arms and legs standing about two inches tall. The managing director, a ruthless employer, drives his staff hard and pushes for the best output rates of his factory. He buys pellets of plastic from a supplier in China and feeds it all into a machine which melts and moulds the forms. He designs the toy himself rather than paying for a professional to create a superior version. There is little point anyway, as the soldiers are distributed to small retailers once a year as part of a Christmas bundle. Who cares if they fall apart? Cheaper product means bigger orders, more sales and less competition.

The end result is this. Thousands of small children are delighted on Christmas morning to get a little soldier in their stocking. Mums and dads are pleased to have found cheap items to stuff into the stocking. The joy quickly dissipates once an arm or leg falls off the little plastic lump, and the toy is soon lost or discarded under the sofa. It's most likely to be dropped in the bin with the mountains of other Christmas waste that fills the wheelie bin on 26 December. Plastic pieces soon find their way to landfill, or worse, into the waterways and into the great oceans while the toxins they release gradually poison our aquatic life and ocean mammals. Back at the factory, the employees are no happier. Their pay cheque remains largely unchanged year on year and their MD is unappreciative and unkind to them for their efforts. Has anyone benefited from this whole debacle? Perhaps the retailer? I doubt it. Once they are known for selling cheap items which fall apart they'll lose custom and the MD of this draconian firm is doomed to failure because he just can't understand that the factory he's running is a pointless scam. Everybody loses.

The other firm in Birmingham is run by a considerate and thoughtful entrepreneur who wants to produce toys for children that will be appreciated for decades to come. He hires a product designer who sits down with him and runs through the brief. They need to create a character that has moveable arms and legs for distribution as a stocking filler. This could be a soldier as a Christmas-themed limited edition unit. They research the market and discover that children love collecting and swapping collectable toys that are small enough to fit in their pockets and school bookbags. The entrepreneur holds a think-tank with primary school teachers, nursery owners, parents and children, and builds a profile of what he thinks children not only enjoy but which can enhance their understanding of the world and our society within it. He looks back into his own childhood and fondly remembers swapping Pokémon, Cabbage Patch Kids and Trolls.

He spots an excellent business opportunity and feels alive and excited. He secures a factory and gathers a small group of key employees. He holds a meeting, provides lunch and presents them with his vision for the new concept he'd like to create for the UK toy market. He and the product designer have designed a range of characters. Each has a different theme. The first is a Christmas soldier with a smiling face and nutcracker-style hat with moving arms and legs. It is a festive toy and is the first in the range. It is intended to launch the brand. Every month, for twelve months, they plan to release another two characters. The entrepreneur engages with his staff and asks them to suggest other characters. They suggest a fireman, a policeman, a nurse, a pilot, a footballer, doctor and a baker. Each with a little brass name and personality tag. One of his employees suggests making a village and ancillary play items to complement the characters and provide the children with a 'set' that they can cherish. The staff are thanked and rewarded.

The entrepreneur contacts a plastics recycling firm and with the agreement of the local schools arranges for recycling machines to be delivered to their car parks which the children and families can bring their recycling to. Each family gets a thank-you note and a discount code for the toy brand from each recycling drop. The children assist with making colourful signs for display on the machines about the journey their plastic recycling takes from their school to becoming a toy in the shops! Over a period of time, the entrepreneur has generated a large part of his raw materials from the recycling machine, fed by the community. He makes up the shortfall directly from the recycling firm. He takes time to develop the first prototype and then tests it. By the time it hits the retailers he's gained positive press through his 100% recycled product philosophy and community involvement. He's also generated a swathe of eager local families who are keen to buy this toy with their discount voucher. The children are enthralled that their recycling has transformed into toys! The launch is a success!

The families and press love the new toy and each month await the release of the next character. Over time, the toys become recognised collectors' items and very few of them ever reach landfill or the oceans. The clever use of consumer waste plastics has solved a problem and created a timeless item that is loved and appreciated, and the staff feel wonderful to be involved in such a project. The entrepreneur is happy and content with his work, safe in the knowledge that he is solving a problem, creating something of value and has a sustainable and long-term business model. This will keep him and his family secure for the foreseeable future.

Over time his brand will become recognised nationally and the toys stocked with all the major retailers. He's making a fantastic salary for himself, earning a substantial profit margin for his shareholders. He'll soon have to enlist another two manufacturers to assist him with increasing his output, providing work for other firms alongside his own. Other manufacturers are aware of his ethos and decide to compete, switching to recycled content and echoing his philosophy. The industry is changing. Who loses?

WHAT IF I FAIL?

Entrepreneurs average 3.8 failures before final success. What sets the successful ones apart is their amazing persistence.

Lisa M. Amos
business and health coach

Now I'm just taking a wild guess here, but I believe there is one major reason why you haven't started your business yet. That weighty question which has made its way into the title of this chapter. I hope you can feel a little reassured when I tell you that failure is an absolute necessity for growth. Failure can teach you more than instant success ever will and failure can be your greatest opportunity for recognising what your limitations are and where your product or idea isn't working. Above all else, failure is not the end. It's just the immediate requirement for the redirection of your focus. In 1895, in the US state of Massachusetts, 32 years after Henry Ford was born, and approximately the same time he would have been hard at work releasing his first car, Buckminster Fuller was born. If I were to document one person in this book who you could take inspiration from, it would be him. For he purposefully lived his life as an example of what one 'average' man or woman can achieve when determined to prove this point. Furthermore, he documented everything in miniscule detail so he could prove it. Also known as Bucky, Buckminster's contribution to humankind is still being realised by many of us who come across his work, his story and his incredible determination to establish what is possible.

Why is he relevant to this book? Well, unlike Ford who discovered where his interests lay and ploughed resolutely and determinately in that direction, Bucky experienced thirteen years of humiliation, abject failure, the death of his father and then first-born child, despair and the contemplation of suicide, before he managed to slingshot himself into incredible success by utilising a clear intention and the integrity to follow his heart. I am sure many of us will feel comforted and bolstered by his experiences, and he remains in the forefront of my mind when I consider what is possible for myself and for you, dear reader.

Buckminster Fuller spent the early years of his life learning from the painful experiences that most people would categorise as failure. As a businessman, he attempted to establish a new form of construction that failed financially after just a few years. He lost all his money as well as the investments from his friends and family. With the loss of his construction company and the birth of his second daughter, Bucky found himself, aged 32, in Chicago with no money, no job, no formal education beyond high school, a reputation as an unsuccessful businessman, and no prospects for the future.

He decided to drown himself in Lake Michigan.

It was then that he had a profound experience that transformed him forever. He realised, while contemplating suicide, that he did not belong to himself and therefore had no right to take his own life. In an instant, he discovered that he, like every human being, belonged to a greater power. So, he decided to embark upon a lifelong journey/experiment to document what one average, healthy person with no college degree and no money could accomplish on behalf of all humankind. Something that could not be achieved by any nation, business, organisation or institution, no matter how wealthy or powerful.

With no real means of supporting his family, he resolved to use the only person available for observation. Himself. During the twenty years from 1927-1947, Bucky threw himself into solving the housing problem and studied how nature worked with fewer resources. He found work for a magazine and continued to study nature and just two years later he'd already made a model of a futuristic, circular-shaped home called the Dymaxion House. This was later made into a full-sized prototype with Beech Aircraft and the United States Government. To cut a long story short, Buckminster Fuller went on to create one of the most recognisable structures on this planet today, the Geodesic Dome. For 56 years, he remained true to his mission and documented every aspect of his life and work, making him the most documented 'ordinary' person in the history of humankind.

Between the moment of his realisation to his death at the age of 88 years old, he:

Was granted 25 US patents
Met Albert Einstein
Published 28 books and thousands of articles
Received 47 honorary doctorates
Was presented with hundreds of major awards
Circled the globe 57 times working on projects and lecturing
Delivered fascinating 'thinking out loud' lectures when he was in his eighties.

Bucky was able to teach by example, showing us with his accomplishments and seeming failures that each of us possesses tremendous gifts that we can contribute to others. And he proved that a person can have a satisfying and comfortable life while making his or her unique contribution to our society. Here's a quote that resonates strongly with me:

'Something hit me very hard once, thinking about what one little man could do. Think of the *Queen Mary* – the whole ship goes by and then comes the rudder. And then there's a tiny thing at the edge of the rudder called a trim tab. It's a miniature rudder. Just moving the little trim tab builds a low pressure that pulls the rudder around. Takes almost no effort at all. So I said, that the little individual can be a trim tab. Society thinks it's going right by you, that it's left you altogether. But if you're doing dynamic things mentally, the fact is that you can just put your foot out like that and the whole big ship of state is going to go. So I said, "call me Trim Tab".'

I thought it important to include Bucky in this book to illustrate how his mental state went from one of despair, through failure and loss, to almost inconceivable success. The study of his life and work illuminates how he shifted his focus from 'me' as an individual to 'humankind' as a collective as he sought to use his life to develop solutions for our entire civilisation through his work. This is what Henry Ford refers to as 'service'. Almost miraculously, he managed to go from being expelled twice from Harvard, to being appointed as Professor of Poetry and then elected to 'honorary membership' on the occasion of the reunion of the class from which he was expelled, some 50 years later.

He states that: 'We are powerfully imprisoned in these dark ages simply by the terms in which we have been conditioned to think.' His philosophy was that we should not believe anything we see, hear, read or are told is true. He felt so strongly about this that he removed the word 'believed' from his vocabulary. Rather, he told us that we should compare aspects of reality against our personal experience and decide what is true for ourselves. So in light of this, I can suggest that you should not believe that you aren't capable of starting your enterprise and must not fear failure but embrace it as part of the learning journey. It is important for you to seek out what is true for you and you alone, and you should follow this path despite what others may think of you or what they have conditioned you to believe.

Before you chalk failure up as a reason to exit and return to the perceived safety of employment, just consider these examples of successful people who have failed:

- Albert Einstein performed poorly at school and struggled to find employment when he graduated from the Swiss Polytechnic Institute. Einstein's father died believing he was a complete failure. Einstein was absolutely heartbroken.

- Colonel Harland Sanders was the founder of Kentucky Fried Chicken (KFC) restaurants. At the age of 65, he found himself penniless. He retired and received his first social security check which was for $105. He started travelling by car to different restaurants and cooked his fried chicken on the spot for restaurant owners. If the owner liked the chicken, they would enter into a handshake agreement to sell his chicken. He was turned down 1,009 times before his chicken was accepted once! By 1964, Colonel Harland Sanders had 600 franchises selling his trademark chicken.

- Thomas Edison is one of the most famous inventors in history with 1,093 patents to his name. However, when attempting to invent a commercially viable electric lightbulb, he failed over 10,000 times. When asked by a reporter how it felt to fail so often, he merely stated:

'I have not failed 10,000 times. I have not failed once. I have succeeded in proving that those 10,000 ways will not work. When I have eliminated the ways that will not work, I will find the way that will work.'

- Walt Disney faced many failures. His first company, Laugh-O-Gram went bankrupt. It wasn't until five years later and after plenty of heartache, that he created Mickey Mouse, and began to experience a small amount of success and fame.

So you see, failure isn't the end. It's a stepping stone to success. Learn from an athlete. It takes a lot of training to become world class in your sport. The gold medal is something you earn after many failures. Not at your first attempt. You learn from failures. They enable you to fine-tune your craft and appreciate your blind spots. Get back up off the ground, dust yourself off, and get back to it. Life will continue for you. Accept that when you get start again, you won't be starting from the beginning. You'll be starting from experience.

BROADEN YOUR FIELD OF VISION AND QUESTION EVERYTHING!

Those who have never seen themselves surrounded on all sides by the sea can never possess an idea of the world, and of their relation to it.

Johann Wolfgang von Goethe

25 years old. That's how old I was when I realised that my teachers had lied to me. More specifically, that our English education system is far from objective. I needed to travel to Cambodia and Vietnam to recognise that 'his-story' which I considered immutable fact at school is simply an 'account of past events' often coloured by those who documented them. I discovered gaps left in my education and recognised that our version of 'his-story' is uncomfortably challenged

when compared to 'their-story'. It's actually really helpful to look at our culture through different eyes in order to gain a balanced perspective of what we are. Could you imagine how we appear through the eyes of an indigenous person? Things get stranger when you broaden that perspective out to other species we share this planet with. How does the otter, the seal, the hippo or the lion see us – as their room-mate on planet earth? How do we impact them? What is our place in the intricate web of life and what is it that we are *actually* here to do? Personally, I believe we have the makings of an incredible guardian species. Assisting and supporting those lower down the food chain than ourselves. We've got a unique and complex brain with the emotional capacity to show incredible acts of kindness and yet we can also be impossibly callous. We have agile and strong bodies which can shape landscapes and we can construct, contain and divert vast bodies of water. How can we be so good, and yet so awful at the same time?

As Terence McKenna, a famous American ethnobotanist once quoted, 'We have the money, the power, the medical understanding, the scientific know-how, the love and the community to produce a kind of human paradise. Yet we're led by the least among us – the least intelligent, the least noble, the least visionary.'

Used wisely, our skills and energy could be of enormous benefit to other species but over the years we've followed our human herd and built an emotional wall around ourselves. We left the table and vacated our place in the mammalian family and then shut our hearts down to protect ourselves from suffering. We've seemingly concealed or dispelled our anguish with apathy and amusement. Surely this is a great loss to our extended family, for such an immensely powerful species to be turned inwards and focused entirely on ourselves. Using our power and skills (for the most part) entirely for our own benefit. Collectively, I think we've *all* forgotten that we're part of something incredibly beautiful and that we have a family to support: our brothers and sisters, the mammals and other creatures, a family of which we're very much meant to be a part. Perhaps this is because our sense of security is no longer tied to the web of life, but instead to our banking system and guided by our politicians. It's hard to accept that we're estranged from our wider family and we are now victims of cognitive dissonance and confirmation bias in our shared anthropocentric reality. Supporting each other through this. Reaffirming the normal. Now acclimatised to our new way of being.

But are we? I think many of us have a sense of unease. Do you?

When I was 25, months before I had reached Borneo, Dave and I travelled from northern Thailand through Laos and Cambodia. Transported for the most part by boat on an enormous river called the Mekong. It was a two-month adventure to reach the southern coast of Cambodia before heading east to Vietnam. The lime-green hues, palm fronds and gently sloping terrain of Thailand's rice paddies gave way to a much more complex landscape. In Laos, the hills transmute into mountains of sheer limestone karst that rises up in giant crags from the impenetrable tangle of deep jungle. There is still a great amount of jungle which hasn't been cleared but tourists are forbidden to explore it. It's not possible to walk into the jungle in Laos without the risk of having a limb blown off. You see, from 1964 to 1973, Laos, although not engaged in any war whatsoever became victim to the heaviest bombardment by the United States, earning the title of the most heavily bombed country in history. Consequently, there are still many unexploded missiles left on the ground. I was horrified to learn that the US pilots simply dumped their ordnance on Laos when they were flying west, making their way back from Vietnam to their military base in Thailand. We saw numerous elephants with their trunks blown off in an animal hospital. Not to mention humans missing limbs and living in poverty. How had I not learnt about Laos at school?

The people of Laos were incredibly special. Gentle, warm, friendly and eager to accommodate western travellers. Their houses are thatched bamboo huts which are elevated up on stilts. We often slept in groups on an elevated bamboo floor covered in reed mats, our sleeping bags cocooned in mosquito nets. Local women would offer to wash our clothes in the stream for a few dollars and present us with enormous catfish from the river or a lean chicken from under their house to cook for dinner. There was little to no electricity. We found our way to '4,000 Islands' which is a riverine archipelago in the Mekong in southern Laos. The air was thick with insects, woodsmoke and the cheerful sound of cicadas, toads and frogs croaking and chirruping in the night air. The village we stayed in had no electricity except for a small diesel-powered generator which was fired up for an hour or two at night. One evening, a small group of indigenous women were gathered near a picnic table as I nervously inched towards them to sit down for dinner. The generator was on and a powerful floodlight was raised up on a pole above the women. It cast its beam across the dining area, lighting it up like a football pitch. One of the women caught my eye and grinned widely at me. I tried to hide my shock when I saw a mouth full of dark purple teeth! Later, I learned that hill tribe people of South East Asia maintain a tradition which is thousands of years old. They chew a seed called the betel nut which turns their teeth purple! I tried to mask my surprise but failed spectacularly when suddenly startled by the sound of an enormous flying beetle as it collided with the spotlight above her head. In the blink of an eye I watched the woman as she slammed her hand down, capturing the beetle which dropped down directly in front of her. No sooner had her hand connected with the wooden table than she brought it back up again and crammed the enormous insect straight into her mouth! I am not exaggerating when I tell you that one long spiny black leg was protruding out of her (still smiling!) mouth as she crunched her remarkably disgusting snack.

I learnt a lot in Laos. I was distressed to learn about injustice and suffering, amidst the most beautiful and gentle of people; but the real education came in Cambodia. This is where I learnt about their murderous leader Pol Pot and his regime the Khmer Rouge. The world's most heinous genocide, perpetrated upon innocent Cambodian civilians between 1975 and 1979. Research from the Documentation Center of Cambodia estimates that the death toll was around 2.2 million. I learnt from the Cambodians that the British government were fully aware of the situation but did nothing to assist. We vacated our embassy office and simply left.

The brutal genocide persisted for four years until they were liberated by the Vietnamese. The matter of Cambodia was discussed at length in the House of Commons in 1990 and online parliamentary records show transcripts which provide a detailed account of their debate and of the fact that not only had we failed to act but we were working on a plan to preserve the Communist leader Pol Pot and thus support the Khmer Rouge.

Distressingly, on three occasions – 1979, 1980 and 1981 – the United Kingdom Government *voted to seat the Khmer Rouge* at the United Nations. On those three occasions at least, the Government gave diplomatic support to the Khmer Rouge, despite the fact that they indiscriminately slaughtered millions in the most brutal and horrific manner.

'Why didn't anyone TELL me?!' I cried, standing in the middle of a burial site on the outskirts of Phnom Penh. One of the many Killing Fields where at least 1.4 million were victims of brutal execution and dumped in shallow graves. To think that our nation had the resources to help but didn't led me to cast doubt upon how I saw our great and benevolent leaders, and this in turn ignited the process of making me question ……… everything. A mindset which has helped me as an entrepreneur. If we're going to offer our work to the world and build meaningful businesses, we must be able to see the world for what it is. Not what our teachers told us it is and not simply what we read in the tabloids. What struggles are people facing, where are there problems which need solving and what if government policy is letting us down in some way, wherever we may be?

This book isn't about picking apart the complexity of our political system but it does make me wonder why our schools aren't teaching more of this. How can we be fully educated if the system is biased? We must recognise that we hold far less knowledge than we perhaps think we do and, in fact, perhaps we shouldn't take our formal education too seriously. This also means, celebrate if you weren't too good at school – some of the best entrepreneurs are poor academics. Some of us came out of school feeling less than adequate and I can honestly tell you that if you were put down by a teacher or told you weren't intelligent then that's something to celebrate! If you have dyslexia or ADHD or are a creative, dreamer or class clown, believe me, you have a superpower. It puts you in the class of the outliers. Celebrate your uniqueness and use it to develop your unique business.

In a world where everyone is thinking in the same way, educated on the same subjects and living in a world of 'normal' you my dear reader must work outside of these parameters. You can't be looking at the existing reality from the perspective of seeing everything as 'normal' and therefore 'good'. Normal is certainly not good at the moment and the current system of industry is choking us all to the point of near collapse. Let's challenge 'normal'.

Our exam systems are merely a test of our memory. We are taught to memorise facts. But, I am not convinced that the facts are comprehensive or objective enough to give us enough of an understanding about the world or indeed our unique abilities to create a better one. The creative arts are seemingly being phased out. I find this baffling. Creativity brings innovation and freedom. It's the creativity in us that enables us to deliver our best work and really challenge the status quo. Does the education system not want us to be changing the world? Ah. There we have it. It would be anarchy, wouldn't it? If all of us rose up and created myriad empires which collectively outshone the current systems. We would likely break the system entirely.

So, take time to look at the world with entirely new eyes. Question everything. Literally. Everything. Why do we live in brick, square houses? Why are the insects declining? Why is the healthcare system addressing symptoms and not causes? What is in our food? What do people need right now and why do we buy what we do? Are there alternatives which could be more affordable and more environmentally sound? How does the world *really* work? Like a child, you need to unlearn everything you simply took for granted and question why each industry operates the way it does. Only then can you see that there could be a whopping great problem which needs a solution. Find the problem, create a solution = make a cracking business!

For example, since beginning my journey, my mind has begun to open up to so many opportunities. The frustrating downside to this is that I have numerous business start-up ideas and simply no time to execute all of them. Interestingly, the more you observe, the more you see and the greater volume of 'aha' moments you'll experience. Presently I can see that almost every sector of industry is damaged beyond repair and needs entrepreneurial reform. Look at each industry, and find fault with it. Then, engineer a solution. I'll give you an example.

Take the funeral industry. A 'normal' industry. Did you know that three quarters of all people in the UK are cremated when they die? Is this a problem? Well, let me see... if you look into this industry, you'll soon discover that one cremation uses as much energy as a 500-mile car trip and releases a toxic cloud of over 250 kg of carbon dioxide (and highly toxic mercury!) vapour into the atmosphere. But, wait. Isn't there a huge 'carbon' issue? And an agenda being led primarily by the government to reduce carbon emissions? Has anyone actually spotted this huge dirty carbon cloud? This is an *enormous* industry considering that there were 543,293 cremations in the UK in 2020 across 310 crematoriums.

Turn this on its head and a much more pleasing solution appears. It doesn't take much brainpower to consider that saving the planet involves planting millions of trees, rewilding open areas and creating wildlife habitats. So, how can we make money from planting trees?

Ditch the cremations. Give people beautiful tree burials. If a thoughtful and proactive entrepreneur wanted to combine trees with burials and create a national chain of forests, working with national charities and tree planting initiatives they could seek a really good future in the funeral industry, creating not only nature reserves, but creating places we'd all like to go when we die ... all the while running this as a business and making money to inter bodies (not embalmed but naturally, of course!) under the saplings of beautiful native tree species and creating a reserve which families and friends can visit. Could you imagine having a picnic under the shade of the majestic tree which has grown from your loved one instead of standing over a boring old gravestone? Imagine, a nation covered in trees again. The final gift we can all give our earth. Our selves. That's something. Burial meadows and forests nourish our soil, capture the carbon and soothe our souls. That's the future I want to share with you.

'It's difficult...' I hear you. You think it's difficult. But in reality, it's not.

Let me tell you why. As a creative entrepreneur you have the idea. Then you develop the business concept and when you've tested it out as a prototype or trial you hire people who enable you to deliver it. A good friend of mine introduced me to an associate of his last year. This chap was a remarkable entrepreneur. He has several successful businesses. One of his earlier businesses happened to be a well-respected law firm.

'Are you a lawyer then?' I asked him naively. He looked at me quizzically. 'No,' he chuckled. 'I built a website, secured an office and hired lawyers.'

This is the job of the creative entrepreneur. You spot your opportunity. Design the business. Brand it. Get your website live. Test the market by establishing a waiting list or a small order book with a waiting list. Develop the concept with a minimum viable product (if you don't know what a minimum viable product is, it's a prototype version of a product with just enough features to be usable by early customers) and then hire your technicians to do the specialist work. Despite what you might think, you don't need to be a mechanic to have a garage any more than you have to be a published author to set up a publishing house. You just need to know what the public needs and create the platform to deliver it.

How do you know if it's the right idea? You'll feel it. It's like falling in love. You'll get an emotional clue. Remember to check in on the emotional self. I experienced a crazy surge of energy when I was in the EcoHab Dome Home on my college field trip. It continued on for quite some time after, as I was driving home in a total whirlwind of excitement. I felt euphoric. It was completely illogical. This was a clear confirmation that I had stumbled across something very important to me. The indicator, for me at least, was a sensation.

Following on from that you will likely experience HUGE coincidences. These are confirmation. You will not believe this when I tell you that three years into my start-up journey, I was having a difficult time between the first company collapsing and the next company being launched. I had suffered my first business set-back and was looking for confirmation that this was still the right path for me. At the time, a friend and I were taking a trip to Hampshire to visit the farm I was raised on. Now a commercial premises, but the farmhouse itself was still there and the new owners happily put the kettle on and walked me round so I could relive my childhood memories. As these things often go, the woman at the house noticed my sign-written van on the courtyard. 'You build roundhouses...?' she asked. I grinned. Before I could launch into a sales pitch, she locked her eyes onto mine, eyes wide, and brought her hand to her mouth whilst wildly pointing her finger towards the window.

'Don't you know about the roundhouse site?!' My jaw must've dropped to the floor!

It turns out that a few years after my family had sold the farm, the new owner was putting a concrete helipad (helipad!) on the field. But they needed planning permission. Lo and behold, a geological survey was undertaken by Oxford Archaeological Unit and they found and documented the site of an Iron Age roundhouse settlement in the field. The field where I spent the majority of my time as a young child, looking for newts in the stream with my brothers and sisters. This was total and complete confirmation, in my eyes. It was all the reassurance I needed to continue onwards. You too will find the most absurd coincidences on your journey. You may have already experienced something like this. Something so bonkers it can't possibly be true. When you see it. Act on it. Know it is a message of encouragement. This type of event happens seldom in our lives.

Open up your field of vision. Travel if you can. Look at the world in a completely upside down way and question it all. Imagine an alternative. Look deep into nature. Your idea will come. When it does. Look out for the energy high! You'll know it when you feel it.

BUT I'M A LAWYER!

You don't become what you want,
you become what you believe.

Oprah Winfrey

'But I am not an entrepreneur!' I hear you cry. 'I'm a lawyer!'

Have you somehow convinced yourself that because you studied law or accountancy when you were at university, this automatically disqualifies you from being an entrepreneur?

The only obstacle you are most likely facing in this situation is that of the velvet handcuffs. This is a situation where your salary and benefits are so attractive that it is unlikely you'll be able to achieve this level of perceived security or lifestyle if you jump ship and decide to embark on a radical life change. The problem isn't the profession you are currently in. It's your willingness to sacrifice your short-term finances to secure a long-term objective of living a life of freedom. If you have a well-paid profession but you're unhappy with the concept of being trapped there for the rest of your life then the issue isn't that you're 'not an entrepreneur' it's that you are accustomed to a lifestyle and you are unwilling to part with it, temporarily. But it is temporary. Take it from me. You will need to look at your expenditure and carefully negotiate with yourself and your spouse as to how you can streamline your life and reassess your priorities. What do you want? Ultimately you have a choice. Stay as you are? Or evolve into the human being you'd like to be? Stretching yourself to your fullest potential and living a life of your own design? Accepting that you will indeed suffer losses to your income for a period of one to three years while you're getting yourself up and running is a powerful mindset and will serve you well. Patience, my friend.

The short-sighted individual will sacrifice their freedoms, while a long-sighted and determined professional will feel the fear and do it anyway. So, you can't go on holiday next year. Deal with that. Once you've weighed up the pros and cons of short-term vs long-term and managed the fear that invariably arises from this, you are well on your way to designing your business and taking total responsibility for your life.

Humans are multi-faceted. We can cook, dance, run, write, paint, calculate, negotiate, drive, dive, fly, become parents... The human psyche is capable of many processes. The choice of career you made a long time ago is not mutually exclusive to the new potential career choice you have in front of you. If anything, this is an excellent string to your bow and further enhances your breadth of skills as an entrepreneur. It's a transition of your career, not the death of it.

To be an entrepreneur simply means that you are bringing something new to the world. You will build a business around your offering. If it's a good idea it will most likely succeed and your business will bring in enough revenue to employ many people and touch the lives of millions. If it's a bad idea, you'll struggle to make money to employ staff and will struggle along (without being paid) until you decide to give up on it and pivot to a new idea. Any professional can step into the arena and show up with their offering. You can draw upon your experience in your profession to leverage your offering and improve the viability of your idea.

Most entrepreneurs will tell you that starting a business was something they always felt destined to do. But a surprising number of 'accidental' entrepreneurs, people who never in a million years thought they'd be running their own business, can be found among the ranks of the self-employed.

A study of entrepreneurs by the Recruit Venture Group found that a third of business owners never planned on starting their own company. In spite of the challenges they faced, from raising finance and finding customers to managing it with little personal income, only 1% regret their decision, while 12% wish they'd started their business sooner. Around 90% say they are happier than when they were employed.

Coffee Republic was founded in 1995 by Sahar Hashemi, OBE and her brother Bobby. Working as a solicitor, she had no idea that she was an entrepreneur. But a trip to New York inspired her. Sahar developed a passion for skinny lattes and cappuccinos and recognised on her return to England that she was missing her coffee fix in London where there were no decent coffee bars like those in the USA. After expressing her annoyance and dismay to her brother (how inconsiderate it was that nobody had thought to open coffee shops in London!) the idea was born. Although she doubted herself capable of being an entrepreneur, she went on to build a national empire of coffee shops. Within five years, the business had 61 cafés in the UK. Sahar exited the organisation in 2001, just six years after building it from scratch. She became a very wealthy woman in the process. So, how can a solicitor with no entrepreneurial experience build one of the largest coffee chains in the UK? Was it an accident? Or was it simply that she had the courage to try?

Sahar published a bestselling book called *Anyone Can Do It* and within it she talks fondly about the fact that she, like me, (and most likely, like you!) is an 'accidental entrepreneur'. She had no desire to leave her profession as a solicitor and was stunned at the notion that she could ever start her own business.

I phoned her during the 2020 lockdown and asked what her thoughts were on the pandemic and whether this would affect anyone considering starting a project in an economic recession. 'Business is all about meeting customers' needs,' she said. 'I founded Coffee Republic in a recession and I do believe that gaps can open up at these times. People will still require products and services even in an economic downturn. Look for the gaps that open up in times of hardship and you will find opportunities. As long as you are meeting the needs of the customers you will have a great business.'

Sahar grew her business exceptionally quickly. Her business model was based on a national network of accessible coffee shops on every street corner. Her core piece of advice? 'As a founder, one of my biggest regrets was stepping away from the business. Many of us believe we have to become corporate but that's a mistake. Keeping the small business mentality is critical. The input of the founder is absolutely critical to a company's success. Don't forget that.'

'We took the leap into entrepreneurship,' says Sahar. 'My belief is that you leap and a net will appear. Everyone said 'no' to us, everyone thought our idea was crazy, including every supplier we spoke to. We went to 39 bank managers and only the fortieth bank manager said they would give us a £90,000 loan to open a coffee bar, because the 39 that rejected us said we were a nation of tea drinkers and we'd be crazy bringing coffee here. We had to bootstrap and be extremely resourceful. We couldn't even find employees to work there because all of the offers that we got were people used to working in greasy spoon cafés. We ended up opening the doors to our coffee bar one year after we'd had the idea. Now, we all know about the huge coffee bar craze. By 2023, there are expected to be 32,230 coffee shops in the UK.

'I don't believe in overnight success. We opened the doors and no-one came in. We had to make sales of £700 a day to break even but for the first six months we were only making £200 a day. The following year we opened one more store and I remember thinking, 'Oh, we're getting to be a big chain now'. But then we went to seven stores, 30 stores, 60, 80, and by about 110 stores we had become a big company. We then thought, "Now we're a grown-up business, it's time to hire great people with great CVs and experience," but the problem was we'd become a big company and had lost that spark we had at the beginning. We weren't customers ourselves any more, we were corporate.

'Sometimes entrepreneurs feel like they have a sell-by date and that it's time to go. Bobby and I both sold our shares at the time and we left, and it was really sad. Emotionally it took a toll on us, leaving a business we started, because we absolutely loved it. I learned a big lesson leaving the business I had started because the market exploded and we didn't leave the company with the right tools, we didn't keep the start-up culture, and we'd grown out of the start-up mentality.

'My biggest lesson then? Act small no matter how big your business is or how big it becomes, maintain that start-up mentality.'

These are Sahar's six business rules to live by:

1 'Make it all about your customers – see your business through your customers' eyes. Think about delighting your customers. "Delighting" seems like a flaky word but

it's a powerful thing to do, as when you think this way all the great opportunities come into view.'

2 'Get out of your office. Don't get stuck down with paperwork. There are so many technology solutions that can do that for you and if you're not getting out there you're not seeing what your customers see.'

3 'Be clueless. When you start a business and you have no idea, it's the biggest advantage because you're not contaminated by how things are or "this is how we do things". Be like a big kid again, don't be afraid to ask questions – adopt an outsider mentality with how things should be done.'

4 'Experiment and bootstrap. Be resourceful and try new things – innovation is all about trying new things; you're going to make a fool of yourself but allow yourself that.'

5 'Give yourself license to fail. When we start a business, we're not perfectionists and we're not terrified of failure. We become more afraid of failure as we build a bigger business but the only way to avoid failure is to do nothing and that's not an option.'

6 'Be 100% yourself – you don't have to become all corporate and be an automaton. It's all about having your head and heart in the business and having fun too.'

She adds: 'Remember, we're in a rapid pace of change; it brings a lot of challenges but the opportunities are huge.

Next time an opportunity comes along and your mindset is right, you're grabbing the opportunity and you're taking the leap and I can *guarantee* a net will be there to catch you.'

NEWSFLASH: YOUR LIFE (AND BUSINESS) ISN'T ABOUT YOU

If you want to lift yourself up, lift up someone else.

Booker T. Washington

Kat is a bright young woman who decides to open up a gourmet cupcake boutique in her local village. She's coveted this dream for many years, imagining all the reasons why having her own shop, bursting with the most delicious cupcakes, would make her life complete. Poring over Instagram images of successful bakeries in London and Paris, she visualises the expensive, delicately-iced cakes which could make her a fortune. Her early days of setting up her first business are exhilarating. She carefully selects all the things that make her happy and give the shop real personality. From furnishings to the menu to the company name (Chicago CupCakes) and delights in the smallest detail. Her life is coming together. The future looks bright for Kat.

Friends and family support her when she excitedly shows them the 'American diner' interior design style she's so fond of. Her passion lies with cupcakes, bright colours and her beloved American pop culture. She's ecstatic. This is perfect. She's destined for success. Everyone is going to love Chicago CupCakes.

The first year of trading, Kat gives it her all. The baffled but delighted early customers arrived at the shop gazing wistfully at the bright décor and the massive array of fluorescent gourmet iced cupcakes and exotic beverages. Kat loves iced tea. She wanted to bring it to another level and supply five different styles to her customers. Tall glasses of flavoured tea and elaborately-iced cakes were served up on red polka dot plates. It was heaven on earth for Kat! She was so incredibly proud of her business.

For the initial few months Kat saw trade on a small but consistent basis. She was taking enough to cover her direct costs but couldn't yet put herself on a salary. She was living off her savings and working around the clock to ensure that her brand and shop were established and turned over enough trade to budget for more advertising. Slowly, and ever so surely the customers started dwindling.

She hadn't changed anything. Her shop was still glistening and dazzling.

After just fourteen months Kat sadly closed her doors. The clients dwindled down to a few family members and her ever-loyal best friend (but, secretly, they too were a little sick of cupcakes).

What did Kat miss? The village she lives in is adjoining a mining town in the North East of England. At its height, the mining industry employed more than a million people, but the closure of North Yorkshire's Kellingley Colliery in 2015 brought an end to deep coal mining in the UK. While unemployment is lower than it used to be, these areas continue to have large numbers of people out of work and on benefits. There are also a great number of elderly residents and their carers. The concept of an elaborate American diner serving exotic cupcakes and over-priced iced tea simply had no relevance to the people of the town. There was just no thread connecting the people and the culture of the town to the offering of Kat's dream. Put simply, she created the dream for herself, but not for the people she was intending to serve. Furthermore, she'd not taken notice of the fact that sugar was starting to dominate the headlines in the UK media. One celebrity chef, Jamie Oliver, launched a nationwide campaign to combat sugar consumption and was working tirelessly through TV and printed media to gain traction for his enthusiastic crusade.

Due to the fact that the national press was busy slamming sugar, many people were starting to consider the implications for their health. The business model Kat was driving was launching at the worst time, for a cultural shift was beginning to form in her country and sugar was fast becoming public enemy No.1.

We all suffer from internal bias. The likelihood is that if Kat loved American diners and cupcakes, she came to the conclusion in her mind that other people would also like these things. Without creating a market analysis or a business plan, the cupcake shop was created around the wishes and desires of just one person. The owner! Unfortunately, this isn't enough to gain traction in many cases and when designing a product or service only one thing needs to be established first. Is there an evidence of need? Who are you promoting your business to? Are they like you? Where are your customers likely to be found and what are their shopping habits? What does the town need and how could they benefit from a new solution or product? If she'd done a thoughtful analysis on her local area, client personality type, and the overall demographic, she might have launched an entirely different business altogether.

Picture another scene:

Robin has a passion for wildlife photography. He travels out to his local nature reserve every Friday where he takes up residence in the bird hide to capture a glimpse of a white stork, heron or kingfisher. If he's lucky he'll spot an otter. They were released here, along with beavers a year or so ago. The reserve is owned by a local utilities company. It's a privately-owned reservoir that feeds three towns nearby. Early mornings and late evenings it is quietest. The busier times are bustling with families, couples, mums pushing prams, and dog walkers meandering along the circular route which encompasses the full six kilometre perimeter of the lake. Thoughtfully, the utilities company installed a disabled-friendly footpath to enable as many people as possible to enjoy this large, glistening body of water, flanked either side by hillsides of heather and deep forests. No matter what the season, the valley is beautiful and is attractive to many.

Robin takes every Friday off from work to be here. He's a family solicitor in the city of Manchester, twenty miles away. He commutes by train and sits in his office all day, secretly wishing he were out here, with others who also share his passion. How this could be possible, he didn't yet know. He is hoping that his wildlife photography will start to sell and he can start off down that route. Beautiful pockets of ancient woodland nestle against rocky outcrops jutting out of the water and enormous pine trees sway in the breeze on the far side of the bank opposite the car park. On many occasions Robin has wished that he could get a hot cup of tea and a bacon sandwich at this amazing place. It's five miles from the nearest town and on the bitterly cold, winter days he needs to leave earlier than he'd like just because he needs to warm up in the car on the way home.

The same irritating thought occurs to him consistently. Nagging at him. Why on earth hasn't someone installed a little café here with a toilet and a place to sit and warm our hands on a cold day? Wouldn't it be wonderful if there was an information booth, or even a little gift shop or a viewing area where one could get a hot sandwich and a coffee before coming back out to the forest for another long spell among the trees? Just a coffee trailer would do really. Just something. He shrugs it off, thinking that it is what it is. Perhaps someone would do it, one day. For many months he retains this mindset, slightly annoyed that nobody has had the sense to do anything...

One Friday morning, he happens to be walking back to his car and a flustered young mum is trying to deal with a furious toddler. Her little red face is streaked with tears and one of her chubby little hands grasps a doll and pram while the other is firmly locked into her mother's. Robin can't do much but look on as the desperately frustrated woman begs her child to come along with a promise of a hot chocolate 'when we get home'. She half-carries, half-drags her inconsolable child in the direction of the car park and Robin remembers again his frustration at not having a hot chocolate available, for this exact situation. Three elderly people are walking across the path in front of him clutching their binoculars. 'Surely they would need somewhere to warm up?' he thinks. Then he notices a dog-walker searching for a bin, clutching a dog bag in one hand, shielding his eyes from the sun and peering out across the path with the other. 'What if the human needed to go too?' he wonders...

And that is it.

Something snaps inside him. He knows that it is his time to take action. Scribbling down the contact details from the sign on the car park at the entrance to the reservoir, he promises to do something about this. He can see, quite clearly now, that there is a need for what he had envisioned.

It's twelve months later. Robin is pulling up to work in the car park of the place he loves most in the world. It's early morning, a thick mist is rising up from the surface of the still lake. A glowing, orange hue emanates from the horizon, sending shafts of warming light through the trees which cast long and beautiful shadows across the still, glassy surface of the water below. He steps out of the car clutching his keys in his hand, and swings his satchel over his shoulder as he crunches across the gravel to the newly-constructed eco-building which sits on the shore. He can hardly contain his excitement as he steps onto the decking which ascends in six shallow steps up to the staff entrance door, and he grasps the smooth wooden handrail that has been crafted from timber selected from this site.

Robin is the proud owner and founder of 'Otters' Holt', a collaboration between the utilities firm and his own company. 'R.D.G. Ltd' (his initials). A beautiful, raised eco-lodge with a fully glazed water-facing elevation and solid timber frame construction, the whole structure sits one metre above the water, sitting on elegant posts which rise out of the water to support a wide, sweeping decking area like a jetty or a pier.

Capable of seating 50 people, Otters' Holt has a café, toilets, a small children's play corner, a wildlife engagement area, and small gift shop.

Robin did something about it.

Robin created something of value for people who visit the reservoir. He has also elevated the reputation of the utilities company and he's making them money and provided a sustainable long-term revenue stream that diversifies their portfolio. He quit his job and devoted himself full time to this project. He has created a place for himself to thrive, immersed in his passion.

How did he do it? He drew up a business plan. He interviewed 250 people he met walking around the reservoir over the couple of months after his 'eureka' moment. He posted a survey through the letterboxes of local homes. He went to the bank. He went to his family. He went to the utilities company. They saw his business plan. They backed it. The utilities company agreed to pay for the building if he would project manage the build, open the café, hire the staff and run it as his own, provided, of course, he uses their branding and finishes it to their desired standard. The profits are split 50/50 with the utilities firm. Rob is running his own project (from a building he designed) which ties in with the ethos of the site. He secured himself a salary. He obtained a grant for the marketing and branding. All parties are happy.

Inside, the café is furnished with natural wood boards and floor-to-ceiling photographs of the wildlife on this reserve. It would appear Robin's wildlife photography has taken off after all! Information about the release of otters and beavers is run alongside the visual imagery, and engagement meetings with the wildlife trusts, the utilities firm and government officials take place there regularly. The public now come to Otters' Holt for a day out and the local dairy farm stocks ice cream which is in high demand in the summer months. The local farms all supply produce to this café, in fact. Robin has made good friends with them all. Robin found not only his passion but that of others around him. He spotted an opportunity and sought to solve a problem for other people. Robin was a success. Not only did the café and information centre thrive, Robin then went on to set up three others at other sites which the utilities company owned in the UK. His business was not about him. It was about solving a need for both the landowners and the public. Robin spread his wings and flew.

This is the difference between designing for a desired need as opposed to designing for your personal wants. This is the way to frame a start-up if you want to succeed. Newsflash: your life (and business) isn't about you! It's about the lives you touch and benefit through the existence of your idea.

TRANSFORM PROBLEMS INTO SOLUTIONS

If you're going through hell, keep going.

Winston Churchill

Whenever you see a problem present itself in your life, stop and think. Listen to what you're saying and transform it into a solution. Rather than make the statement, 'It won't work because of....', flip this around into, 'How could I get around this?' or 'What would make this work?' Looking at situations from a solution perspective can give you insight and enable you to resolve a flaw in your business model. This can work on a personal level as much as it does in business. Never be afraid to pivot. If your price is too low, just increase it. A living, breathing business is better than a dead one because the founder was too afraid to disrupt the process for their few customers in the early stages.

For example: I recently tried to make some progress in my garden. It was hopelessly overgrown. The previous resident had lived here for a decade without once going in there. Armed with some loppers and pruning shears, I set to work with enthusiasm, crashing in through the deep nightmare of hawthorn, half-collapsed trees and brambles which encircled me. A few hours of this resulted in a mountain of branches and twigs in the centre of my garden. I spent hours heaving them into the back of my work van and to the local tip. I was knackered. Weeks went by and I was only just starting to see sunlight. With every passing day the mountain of twigs and branches grew and grew and grew. Before too long it was a towering monster that filled my garden. It was not a twig pile any more. It was Mount Etna in all her glory. It sat there for months. Every now and again, another branch would be flung onto the summit. I had a pathway in, a loop around the mountain and then a pathway out. Week after week I would make excuses as to why I couldn't possibly load anything into the van. 'It's too big,' I'd whinge. 'It'll take me a hundred trips,' I'd moan. The mountain kept growing and the excuses kept flowing. I was really quite stuck, exasperated and, quite frankly, paralysed.

One day, when trying to squeeze my way between Mt Etna and the perimeter fence of my garden, I flipped. 'I've had enough!' I ranted. 'How can I solve this? What do I need to make this go away?' The excuses stopped. In my mind was a satisfying image of a big trailer, a lorry, or a tractor to scoop the whole thing out of my garden and out of my life forever. My pleasing daydream turned into a dark ominous cloud once more. 'But I don't have access to any of these things...'

The feeble excuses were starting to return. I switched back to solution-based thinking. If I didn't have a tractor, who did? My neighbour. A dairy farmer who lives half a mile away. He has a son who's a university student and might appreciate some cash. Within minutes, I'd spoken to the farmer, explained the problem, and a week later his son came trundling over with his tractor and trailer and the whole problem just disappeared in a few hours. OK, so I had to pay for this but it was a quick buck for him and it solved my problem. Win-win situation. Why hadn't I seen this solution months ago? I needn't have spent months moaning and procrastinating about this ridiculous situation when I had a solution there all along. I just needed to stop and visualise the solution first. Remember, always approach a problem with, 'How can I make this go away? What do I need?' Focus on the solution. Imagine an image of the solution – dream it up – then take steps to get there.

Solution-based thinking is the hallmark of some very successful people. Just one single impulsive act can be the spark of creativity from which then grows an international organisation. The mere act of visualising a simple solution to a problem which is immediately facing you and then working backwards from there can deliver a powerful result. A prime example of this is how Richard Branson started his airline.

In 1984 Richard Branson was stuck at the airport, trying to leave Puerto Rico for the British Virgin Islands. His flight had been cancelled and he was frustrated, stuck, and away from his girlfriend. 'I was livid because I hadn't seen her for three weeks,' Branson recalled in an interview for a CNBC podcast.

Branson, undeterred and seeking a solution, marched to the back of the airport, gave them his credit card, 'hoping it wouldn't bounce', and hired a plane. He then worked out how much each seat would cost each passenger, borrowed a blackboard, wrote as a joke, 'Virgin Airlines one-way: $39 to the Virgin Islands', and filled up the flight with all of the other delayed passengers.

'When we arrived in the BVI, somebody said, "Sharpen up your service a bit and you could be in the airline business,"' Branson recalled. 'So the next day I rang up Boeing and said: "I've just had a bad experience and I'm thinking of starting an airline called Virgin. Do you have any second-hand 747s for sale?"'

Shortly afterwards, a Boeing representative named R. J. Wilson met with Branson to discuss his airline ambitions. Wilson was not convinced by the name Virgin. But he was convinced by Branson, and agreed to lease him the second-hand 747 aircraft for a year while he tried to get the business off the ground. Richard Branson has shown, from chartering his first aircraft to creating a fully-fledged airline, that honest and authentic problem solving can bring about a genuine business concept. He said when he was branding Virgin Atlantic that someone told him, 'Nobody, nobody, will ever fly on an airline called Virgin'.

Your 'airline' moment might very well be a solution you happen across when presented with a frustrating problem in your day-to-day life. Richard Branson is not superhuman. He is not an alien. He is a human being like you and I, with imagination and courage which enable him to seek solutions to problems. Could you summon up the courage to act impulsively and seek a solution for yourself and others? As he did? This, as far as I can see, is how a great business often starts. Don't have the capital for an aeroplane? Scale this down a bit, and you could start a community project or a small limited company for a small amount and grow it slowly.

In the most recent UK coronavirus lockdown of 2021, I accidentally created a second-hand bookshop with the help of a friend of mine. This was a wonderfully fortuitous side-effect of an impulsive lockdown experiment: a small-scale book delivery service called 'BookBox'. This was a simple solution to a problem I personally faced due to the coronavirus restrictions. Whilst everyone around me was bemoaning the restrictions, from my perspective they actually opened up quite a few opportunities for diversification within businesses or gaps for new start-ups.

So, I needed to first identify a problem to be fixed. As it happened, there was an enormous problem sitting, quite literally, under my nose.

Whilst shopping on Amazon.co.uk one night and gleefully dropping more titles into my shopping basket, I was suddenly struck by the sobering fact that I was spending an obscene amount of money on new books. The children had bookcases crammed with storybooks we'd read ten times over and the shelves were starting to bow under the weight of yet more which had been squeezed onto the ever-increasing mass of titles. Furthermore, I wondered, how many other people in my local neighbourhood had the same titles on their shelves which were gathering dust, and could they be experiencing the same problem?

People like myself are fantastic donors to their local charity shop, arriving with boxes and bags overflowing with practically new books many times over the course of one year. This, for the most part, is not because we are particularly aligned with the charity itself, but as a fundamental requirement for survival. We simply must keep making room for the next tsunami of titles, often riding the Royal Mail or courier wave in hundreds of cardboard sleeves, boxes and jiffy bags. This is a grave situation indeed. You see, a book lover in a lockdown situation could wind up literally drowning in books and their associated packaging materials. Bombarded with the ever-increasing delivery of new purchases brought on by either boredom or late-night book-binges after a glass of wine ... we are the invisible victims of the coronavirus pandemic. I was facing this very real crisis on a personal level. There was no outlet!

With the charity shops shut, I was facing overflowing shelves and bored children. Couple this with too much money being spent online and a recycling bin which can't accommodate the mountain of empty boxes sitting in my porch. I needed a solution. I just wished for someone to enter my house, sweep all of the books off the shelves and deliver me a reasonable bundle of good quality, nearly-new books in exchange.

One morning in mid-December I heard the clatter of the milkman, collecting empty bottles and delivering a new supply. An idea popped into my mind. A book-round.

I just collect a box of books each week from other people like myself. At the same time, a selection of books based on the preferences of the householder could be delivered as a new supply. A simple premise really. Books in. Books out. I thought I'd run with it as an experiment.

Remember Sahar Hashemi, the contributor from the earlier chapters? She produced an interesting podcast explaining how first-time entrepreneurs should create a 'shopping list' of the elements one would need to start a business and work from there. So, what would someone need to start a book collection and delivery service?

A warehouse/lock-up and associated shelving/storage
A van (or a milk float?) and driver
Boxes??
A computer or laptop to keep inventory
A phone
Website
Marketing material
Books – really high quality books – practically
new in fact.

Over the past twelve months, I spent some of my spare time as a volunteer director for a small community project in my local town. The organisation looks after a derelict Heritage Warehouse in the centre of the town, owned by the Canal & River Trust. The aim was to restore this building and open it to the public for events and markets. The main figurehead in this social enterprise is a chap called Neville Clarke, usually seen around town with his collie dog, Ellie.

He is always looking for ways to be more accessible to the community and connect with people in the town.

Bingo! A warehouse. A landmark in the centre of the community. Somewhere that people can walk and drive to. What next? A van. I have access to a work van. It's a little zippy Berlingo with Roundhouses vinyl-wrapped down each side and the strapline, 'Life's too short to be boxed in'. The fact that my van openly dislikes boxes simply had to be brushed aside. Beggars can't be choosers. I now had two of the core components required to start this little enterprise.

So, I called Nev and ran through the idea.

Nev was in. He was happy for me to base the operations in the warehouse. He wanted to join me. He was secretly drowning in books too. He had reached the point where he could no longer open his front door for the books piled up behind it. I then realised that this was a humanitarian crisis on a national scale. We needed to get to work, immediately. So. Stock next. Books. I needed to put a call out to every household in the region. Darren, a local graphic designer created a logo in less than 48 hours. I set up a very simple website with the mission and the concept. (Less than 70% there...!)

BookBox was designed as a not-for-profit. I love the idea 'entrepreneurial activism' but most people call this 'social capitalism'. It is my belief that we can all make profits through our businesses, but we can choose to divert some of those profits to causes we care about rather than merely to shareholders' pockets. When it comes to job satisfaction, the act of doing something worthwhile with your profits can pack a powerful punch in the happiness department. So, I spoke to the Derbyshire Wildlife Trust. They granted me use of their logo if I donated a percentage of our revenue to them. I was delighted! The logo sits alongside ours on the website and on the marketing material. Everyone loves the Wildlife Trusts. This brought us two benefits. It gives the brand more credibility which allows us to achieve more donations plus it gives us more motivation to make it work – because this scheme is actively helping a much beloved wildlife charity.

6,000 leaflets were hurriedly designed, printed and dispatched immediately to the Royal Mail distribution centre. They delivered these to every door in a three-mile radius. 'The Milk-round for your mind!' it declared. 'Books wanted' and 'Free collection!'. Coupled with the Derbyshire Wildlife Trust logo and a 'Books for Biodiversity' message, it illustrated that this was an initiative to raise money for the environment and rotate books simultaneously. Just two weeks later, we came to the warehouse one morning to find a queue of cars waiting at the warehouse entrance and my phone ringing off the hook with collection requests. By the end of the month, Nev and I were unable to see each other through the towering stacks of immaculate books which filled every available surface in the warehouse. There were so many people who were desperate to re-home their books.

The subscription scheme filled up with customers and when we'd reached over 30 local subscribers I knew the project had real potential on a larger scale. At this point, I'd sunk about £1,500 of my savings on a website, leaflets, racking, fuel and boxes. But, we'd gained a steady stream of subscribers, had a fully-stocked (overstocked!) bookshop and tens of thousands of pounds worth of stock. Capitalising on what the charity shops were doing (shutting their doors), we decided to do the opposite and *open ours.* The public seemed to enjoy gifting their books to us as much as we enjoyed collecting them. As the restrictions eased and the country opened up again, we stopped doorstep delivery and instead declared the warehouse, 'A charity bookshop' instead. Today, the bookshop is still going strong and is providing a salary for two members of staff and continuing to generate long-term additional revenue for the social enterprise so they can further their work.

So, next time a problem presents itself to you. Stop for a minute. Think to yourself, 'What would I like to see instead?!' Let an *image of the solution* pop into your mind. No matter how ridiculous this image might be, it could very well be the seed of a new business venture.

If a milk bottle can inspire the creation of a bookshop, I wonder what could pop up for you?

ALIGN YOURSELF WITH YOUR MISSION

All success begins with **definiteness of purpose,**
with a clear picture in your mind
of precisely what you want in life.

Napoleon Hill

Let's rewind a little to chapter five, when you were visualising your dream scenario. Can you hold a picture in your mind of the 'you' in your dream scenario? The 'you' in your very best, most incredible life?

If you are struggling with imagining yourself in the future, instead take yourself back to your past. The 10 or 11-year-old child you once were. See the world though those young eyes again. Remember what you liked to do. What were your interests? If you were to speak to siblings, parents, childhood friends, what would they say about you? Were you playful? Creative? Mischievous? Did you create things, build dens, write or sing? What did you love? What did you spend the most time thinking about? Can you recall a school project which really engaged you? If you were fortunate enough to have had parents who identified and supported your passions, you'll have a head start. The vast majority of us won't have had parents who encouraged or supported our talents and interests (for they were most likely busy pursuing their own) or will have been pushed in a direction that was chosen for us through their biases and societal projections of what success meant to them.

It is my personal belief that most people in the western world are working in the wrong profession. You are most definitely in the wrong profession. You know this. Now you're aware of it, you can adopt your first entrepreneurial trait and *pivot*. Accept your losses quickly. Accept that you've been in the wrong job without remorse, guilt, despair or any other negative emotions, so you can redirect your focus with determination and embrace the short-term disruption. You are like an athlete training for a gold medal. Training will be painful. You have the end goal in sight. Keep it in your mind and move towards it. Even if it *feels* like you're going backwards, or starting again. The fact that you know you want to change and are steering yourself in a different direction places you light years ahead of those who are still unaware that they are in the wrong job. You aren't going to go backwards. You are transitioning. This is the most important step in your career. Knowing when to quit, as excruciating as this might be, is the only way to secure long-term, genuine success.

'But what if I don't have an idea?! What if it doesn't work?! What if I can't?' Your lizard brain is of course panic-stricken and terrified. Well, let's see. Perhaps if you can figure out your ultimate objective (mission) and then reverse-engineer it, the idea will emerge. Couple this with the skills you have (or suspect you might), a new window of opportunity could emerge out of nowhere. One of the most incredible advantages of being an entrepreneur is the ability to traverse industries. If you become too fixated on a company or a product, you could shoehorn yourself into one small segment and fail to recognise other opportunities. You could call your mission your aim, your objective, your reason for living, your crusade, your reason to get out of bed in the morning. Whatever. Just – what is it that you are aiming for? Most importantly, why?

Let's suppose that in your dream scenario you are an internationally acclaimed movie star or celebrated musician, I would imagine that you are seeking the fame and fortune that comes with this? If you were to achieve success with this dream, what or who would you be once the cameras were moved away and the lights were dimmed at the end of an event or tour? What would your thoughts be? What would you *do* with all of that money? 'Well, er, I'd buy a yacht!' you'd proudly exclaim. 'I'd live in a seafront apartment in Miami! I'd have a Hummer and a castle and I'd spend my time at lavish parties and events!'

You'd likely impress upon me all of these outrageously fun and hugely expensive lifestyle choices but still I'd ask... 'But, who are you, really, underneath all of that?' and 'What's it all for?'

When you really think deeply about what you want fame and fortune for, what conclusion might you come to? It's to achieve happiness, isn't it? If you could be on that yacht or in that beachfront apartment you'd be truly happy, wouldn't you? If so, fantastic! Just proceed to write this mission down and strive for that. But many a wealthy person will tell you that happiness might not lie in wealth alone. One such person is Tom Shadyac. Tom is an American director, screenwriter, producer and author. Shadyac is widely known for writing and directing the comedy films *Ace Ventura: Pet Detective, The Nutty Professor, Liar Liar, Patch Adams,* and *Bruce Almighty*. In 2010 he produced a film entitled *I Am* and he explains that his success brought him unimaginable wealth but he struggled with mental health following on from a bicycle accident in 2007. Shadyac subsequently gave away his fortune, opened a homeless shelter and simplified his life. He sold his Los Angeles mansion and moved into a trailer park. This might seem ludicrous to those of us who'd quite like the mansion and the wealth but, his reasoning behind it all was to find ultimate happiness. In the film, Shadyac conducts interviews with scientists, religious leaders, environmentalists and philosophers including Desmond Tutu, Noam Chomsky, Lynne McTaggart, Elisabet Sahtouris, David Suzuki, Howard Zinn and Thom Hartmann. The film asks two questions: *What's Wrong With the World?* and *What Can We Do About it?* It's a thought-provoking film and if you were keen to explore why a wealthy, celebrated successful person might just abandon it all and produce a film explaining his reasons for doing so, I'd certainly recommend it.

If you are, genuinely, thinking of becoming a musician, you might benefit from listening to the advice of George Harrison, MBE. Harrison was an English musician, singer-songwriter, music and film producer who achieved international fame as the lead guitarist of the Beatles.

'I remember thinking I just want more. This isn't it. Fame is not the goal. Money is not the goal. To be able to know how to get peace of mind, how to be happy, is something you don't just stumble across. You've got to search for it.'
George Harrison

So, we are back to happiness again. The reason this book is entitled the 'joyful' warrior and not 'business' warrior, is because I believe that once you've redirected your life in accordance with your skills and your values then you will be (mostly) in a state of joy. Of course, being a successful entrepreneur means making money too, so I guess if it is financial success you are also after, you *can* actually have it all.

When it comes to an entrepreneur who followed their *mission* to unquestionable success, I shall now take this opportunity to embark on an elaborate sermon about the late Anita Roddick, DBE. Founder of the English high street shop which became an international company, The Body Shop. Decades ahead of her time, she built an international business which continues long after her death. What is wonderful about Anita, is her humanness. An open-minded activist, an intelligent and caring woman who wanted to do business differently. Business which aligned with her values. A business which was actually a *mission.*

She was what I like to call a Joyful Warrior, or an Entrepreneurial Activist. The true embodiment of someone who went out into the world as an inexperienced young woman with nothing but passion for making change happen and a vision for the future she'd like to create. As a humanitarian and traveller, she was a free spirit who started a business to campaign for causes she cared about through the vehicle of business.

My motivation for going into the cosmetics business was irritation, she writes in her autobiography 'Body and Soul'. *I was annoyed by the fact that you couldn't buy small sizes of everyday cosmetics and angry with myself that I was always too intimidated to go back and exchange something if I didn't like it. I also recognised that a lot of the money I was paying for a product was being spent on fancy packaging which I didn't want. So, I opened a small shop to sell a small range of cosmetics made from natural ingredients in five different sizes in the cheapest possible plastic containers. I honestly believe I would not have succeeded if I had been taught about business.*

Anita shocked many passers-by with her enormous displays of animal rights posters and humanitarian aid campaigns. Within her, she held the burning fire of indignation and the desire to use her energy to create a business that aligned with her belief system. While nobody is perfect, Anita was a start-up entrepreneur who was honest about her mistakes and kept her heart on her sleeve as she entered the business world as a novice who, just like you, wanted to start a business which reflected her vision. She was unapologetically authentic.

Anita was steadfast in her beliefs against animal testing and human rights. Her enterprise flourished, not despite the intention behind it, but because of it. In 2004, her one shop had grown to 1,980 stores with 600 products and more than 77 million customers worldwide. The Body Shop was voted one of the top 30 brands in the world and hailed as the second most trusted brand in the UK. Anita Roddick was very open about the fact that she didn't like the beauty industry. She wrote, in her book *Body and Soul*:

I hate the beauty business. It is a monster industry selling unattainable dreams. It lies, it cheats, it exploits women. Its major product lines are packaging and garbage. It is no wonder that Elizabeth Arden once said that the cosmetics business was the 'nastiest in the world'. To me, the whole notion of a 'beauty business' is profoundly disturbing. What is beauty? I believe beauty is about vivaciousness and energy and commitment and self-esteem rather than some ideal arrangement of limbs or facial features as celebrated in fashion magazines and beauty pageants.

So how, one must ask, did one woman who despised the industry go on to start this enormous empire? And what was her secret?

I knew nothing about business when I opened the first Body Shop in 1976. The vocabulary of business was part of a language I did not speak. I certainly had no ambitions to start a big interna-

tional company. I didn't want to change the world, I just wanted to survive and be able to feed my kids. The extent of my business acumen went no further than the grim knowledge that I would have to take in £300 a week to stay open.

To me, what is wonderful about The Body Shop is that we still don't know the rules. Instead, we have a basic understanding that to run this business you don't have to know anything. Skill is not the answer, neither is money. What you need is optimism, humanism, enthusiasm, intuition, curiosity, love, humour, magic and fun – and that secret ingredient, euphoria. None of this appears on the curriculum of any business school. One thing that I have learned is that you have to be true to yourself. At The Body Shop we have done it our way. Our success has been a combination of happy accidents, the right people, good products, an honest approach – and of course, the right values.

PERFECTIONISM VS PROCRASTINATION

'Just Ship It' – like Seth Godin

Business is a combination of human energy and money. To me that equals power. I would go so far as to say that business is the most powerful force in society today.

Anita Roddick

As an entrepreneur, you need to act quickly and sometimes quite impulsively. This can feel uncomfortable until you learn to feel at ease with the fact that your work needn't be perfect. It just needs to be 'out there'. The longer you sit on an idea, the less likely it is to be launched into the world. Many times, I have had ideas which I've taken to 50% launch and then just lost the momentum, got distracted by family or work and the idea just dissolves into the ether, waiting to be revived, even though the likelihood is that it won't.

I can assure you that the most pernicious obstacle that you will most likely face is your own procrastinating mind! This book, which I have procrastinated over for three years now, is only in your hands right at this moment because I refused to allow myself to let this drift into the ether as so many other ideas have. To give you the strength, encouragement and gentle guidance to embark on your own business adventure is the most thrilling prospect for me. I know that: more of us out there in the world giving it our all for absolute freedom is going to change the face of the planet in unimaginable ways. It's up to us to claim our lives back and this is the way to do it. So, please, don't sit on your idea for three years! Don't sit on it for two minutes!

Jeff Bezos, founder of Amazon, operates on something he calls the 70% rule, that 'we're gonna go live with a product when we get 70% there. We are never gonna wait for 90, 95 or 99%'.

In industry, this is usually referred to as the MVP. Minimum Viable Product.

The art of getting things done or avoiding procrastination sometimes boils down to taking swift decisive action before you find a way to talk yourself out of it. The lizard brain will most often try to find ways to avoid making decisions and given more than a few minutes of procrastination will swiftly move on to another interesting thought or opportunity such as sitting down to check Facebook or load the dishwasher.

Mel Robbins' book, *The 5 Second Rule* explains her theory on how we can banish the procrastination that we all fall prey to, and recognise these signs so we can act quickly with tools and solutions to improve the efficiency of our lives. She believes that procrastination is not a reflection of your attitude, work ethic or competence, but is a behaviour meant to help us cope with stress. Whatever we are putting off is linked to something that is stressing us. So we try to avoid the stress and instead seek near-term satisfaction, or at least a distraction from the activity. Thus escaping the stress and experiencing immediate pleasure instead.

What we are avoiding isn't the task but rather the stress that we are associating with the task.

Her '5 Second Rule' is simple. If you have an instinct to act on a goal, you must physically move within five seconds or your brain will kill it. The moment you feel an instinct or a desire to act on a goal or a commitment, *use the Rule*. When you feel yourself hesitate before doing something that you know you should do, count down (as if you are on a rocket launch-pad!!) 5 – 4 – 3 – 2 – 1 – GO!!! and take action immediately.

If you do not take action on your instinct to change, you will stay stagnant. You will not change. But if you do one simple thing you can prevent your mind from working against you. You can start the momentum before the barrage of thoughts and excuses hits you at full force. It might sound overly simplistic but, try it, or seek out her book or her YouTube channel to discover whether her work could be helpful to you and your start-up!

Making split-second decisions is a skill you'll need to master. You will often get it wrong. But in these mistakes come learning opportunities. The saving grace of a good entrepreneur is the ability to pivot. For example, imagine you start out by promoting your new 'low-sugar but vibrantly-coloured pink sherbet fizz' to elderly people who have adventurous tastes. You're making rounds at the nursing homes and doctors' surgeries. Somehow and inexplicably it fails to succeed. It's a crisis, a disaster, a total shambles. You are naturally mortified. What would a pivot mean to you in this situation? That you recognise that this particular target market isn't right.

Take a step back and refocus your attention on a more suitable demographic. Now you've seen a glaringly obvious market. You jump straight back in, this time relaunching it to children who love fizzy flavours and bright colours. Being low sugar you've got a greater chance of reaching them through the shopping activities of their parents who want to protect their teeth. Hey presto!

With a pivot here or there, your product has gained traction! That's a pivot. Disaster averted! You might need to pivot several times when you launch your first concept, but don't be disheartened, it's the twists and turns in the road that bring you success and take you to where your product or service is meant to be.

Being an entrepreneur means that you need to work with many uncertainties. Some ideas might fly, others will not. But you need to exhaust all possibilities. Try everything you can, switching and pivoting at every dead end you reach until you find the key that fits.

Delving into other great business books, it's evident that the really great entrepreneurs just 'do it' and deal with the consequences later. If you genuinely feel that there's a good opportunity and you've done enough research to satisfy yourself that there is evidence of need for your concept, then don't delay. Act quickly. Impulsively. Like an entrepreneur. Don't wait until you're 99% there, get to 70% and go for it.

How many businesses might you go on to create? I have recently come to understand that there is a misconception that successful people have more opportunities. I don't believe they do. I believe that many successful people have acted on a larger percentage of opportunities. Richard Branson has founded over 400 companies, some of which fell by the wayside while others gained momentum. You could easily go on to create multiple businesses. Some may fail but believe me when I tell you that some will undoubtedly succeed. The more chances you take, the higher the odds will be stacked in your favour. How many opportunities or ideas are available to you at this precise moment?

Your lizard brain has of course found a reason to convince you that you're not ready, that you might need to do more research, that you need stability, or that you simply don't have time. If you ever do finally manage to coerce your subconscious mind into giving you a break and allowing you to become the best version of yourself, then you will find that procrastination can arise in a more sophisticated form of disguise. Perfectionism. This one is a killer. It's very common for a desire to make your new business/product or service so right for your target market that you fail to make it to market at all.

Many years ago, I became friends with an exceptional architect. He had a vision for a more sustainable future and committed himself to the launch of his glamorous flat-pack eco-home which would serve society by solving a myriad of problems, from reducing CO_2 emissions to providing compact, healthy housing for first-time buyers.

'That light switch needed to be 50 mm to the left,' he sighed wistfully, looking somewhat dissatisfied as he showed me around his pristine demonstration eco-home one day. 'And this ... this state-of-the-art interface system cost ten times more than a standard one but I found it important to ensure the finishes were ... exceptional,' he explained with a wave of his hand as he wandered off looking for other non-existent problems with his immaculate show home. It really was, immaculate.

While admiring the 100% non-toxic paper-based insulation in the walls and the light sensor taps in the bathroom, I realised that he had designed a 'micro-home' for the environmentally conscious but finished it to the standard of a penthouse suite in an uber-trendy city hotel, well suited to someone with very expensive tastes. His tastes, to be precise.

It was a home fit for an architect. But would it be affordable to an average person like you and me?

He was simply so entrenched in architectural details which the average layperson would not have appreciated. This resulted in procrastination, delays and distraction when it came to getting the actual building sold and shipped off to its new, delighted customer.

It's just too easy to become embroiled in the process of redesigning your product several hundred times before you feel brave enough to launch it. Or, burying yourself in books like these before you actually decide to do something about starting a business. And, when you do, you will likely spend so long agonising over the brand, website and product aesthetics that you might struggle to get out there and communicate passionately to the customers who are waiting to hear from you! Don't hide yourself away in the details. Think Big. Get an early prototype of your product (or a trial version of your software, a free taster session of your service) and just get out and try it out on a real life person! You can start to work on the detail when you release the second and third versions, I promise.

NB. Besides, if your project fails to work, you might have invested, literally, years of your life on a total non-starter. All the more reason to test the concept early – when you're 70% there. You are also making a head start on your competition, if there is any. If it is going to work, you'll get the feedback you need from your first clients and you can improve as you go. You can discount the early orders on the basis that they are prototypes or trial versions; this could be a great compromise for both your peace of mind, and your customer's pocket. (Unless you are planning on producing aeroplanes, life-saving medical equipment, parachutes, deep-sea diving gear or space rockets – in which case, please disregard this entire chapter!)

You can spend decades tweaking the website, playing with design ideas, and shifting colour schemes around. But in order to have a business you need sales. Your early customers won't expect to get the MK9 version of the product. MK0 or MK1 is fine. There will be prototype issues. There might be a dodgy logo. But look where the Ford Fiesta started out and look what it is now. Don't perfect. Just launch it.

What if you get criticism? Well, firstly. Memorise this: 'Never accept criticism from someone you wouldn't go to for advice or someone whose life you wouldn't want to be living!' A negative projection coming from one outside person bears little significance to the viability of your idea. Not everyone will get it. No matter how good an idea is, there are bound to be people with whom it just doesn't resonate. Of course, listen to feedback. Take a balanced view but don't lose heart if you receive criticism; instead, forge this into your manifesto – *prove them wrong*!

Your clients will be observing your start-up from an entirely different perspective to you. Will this product save me time/improve my health/make me money/enable my grandma to get to the shops? The website/phone service/brochure/product might require improvement (and it always will) but in the grand scheme of things, perfectionism is the death knell for your start-up. It will cost you more money, lose you time, and ultimately narrow your reach for your target market. The broader your reach, the more chance you will have of enquiries and then subsequent conversion of these leads into sales which bring you both revenue and ongoing success for your business.

The time you're spending tweaking, toggling, fine-tuning and obsessing is time you're NOT out there selling the damn thing you've created. Become a sales person and get out to where your clients are likely to be found. Start selling, as soon as you possibly can. Your early days are critical for finding your early adopters and getting your business idea noticed and validated. You'll need to spend most if not all of your time marketing and selling your concept.

And then it comes to marketing? Remember: PR and Marketing are *not* sales.

Start with the Marketing. Fine-tune the product offering as you go.

Marketing speaks to the soul. It's a set of values. A symbol of your mission – it reaches out and hooks the attention of potential clients. It's a message to the world. In the message is your value.

Here's an example:

A corporate accountancy firm which helps small businesses might think to advertise themselves with glossy photos of their corporate executives standing in front of the head office with the strapline,

'40 years of experience, using the latest software, ensuring accurate accounting, having exceptional customer service. Never miss a deadline – Trust Us – We are ACE Accountants Inc.'

Meh ... pretty uninspiring, huh?

But how about we spin this on its head?

A clever marketer talks to the customer, from their perspective. They turn the camera around to capture the client, *not* their business. Imagine instead, a lifestyle shot of a family man, in his garden on a hot summer's day, playing with his children; can you see the glistening water droplets of a sprinkler frozen in mid-air over his head as he laughs hysterically at the three children who are clambering all over him? Rays of sunlight are shining through and reflecting off the azure water in the paddling pool, the children have their heads back, shrieking with delight. A BBQ is in the background and the sunlight streams through the leaves of the tree which frames the shot.

The strapline reads, 'We take care of your accounts, so you can take care of what's important to you.' BOOM! They nailed it.

The potential client can relate. They don't *want* to be sitting in front of a spreadsheet – they want to be enjoying their life! They are excitedly picking up the phone, dialling in the number on the advert and visualising how fabulous their life will be once they've delegated their accounts. Oh how they NEED this accountant!! That marketing has worked. It should entice the viewer to pick up the phone and say, 'Yes, please! I need you!' Thus, translate to an enquiry. The enquiry will then go to your 'sales' department (most likely, you) and it's your job to present the price and service and communicate the benefits of your service and sell it to them as a lifestyle change.

Always think of your customer's perspective before your own. It makes a huge difference.

FAILURE TO PREPARE IS PREPARING TO FAIL

It is impossible to live without failing at something unless you live so cautiously that you might as well not have lived at all, in which case you have failed by default.

J. K. Rowling

It was in early December 2014 that the wheels fell off. Actually, they didn't fall. They imploded in a ball of flames so intense that my very life splintered into a thousand shards of utter, inconsolable despair and anguish. Sitting at my desk with five members of staff bustling around me in the office, and a further six men in the workshop. I felt the whole world spin on its axis as the exasperation, frustration and fear rippled through me. 'Written without prejudice', the email was entitled. 'We will not be paying our invoice', it continued. There was no denying that I'd hit rock bottom. Total, undeniable, indisputable cataclysmic collapse. My fledgling company was not yet three years old but had rocketed directly into fifth gear from first and hadn't taken the time to establish its foundations. The whole business was crumbling around me and there was no way out.

It all started well. Orders were indeed flowing in. The small business start-up loan I'd applied for two years earlier had come in soon after the first few orders, and with it, lots of PR from the finance company. In late October, George Osborne, (at the time, the Chancellor of the Exchequer) had swept regally into my office with his numerous entourage and bodyguards, arriving in blacked-out Range Rovers, closely followed by Regional and National News TV vans and media outlets from far and wide. The government at the time was interviewing female-led start-ups working in predominantly male-dominated industries. My neighbours on the industrial estate watched on, mouths agape when they saw the media swarm congregate outside of my humble joinery workshop. The only vans we usually get around that side of the estate surrounded by people are filled with sandwiches at lunchtime. Positive PR was flowing over our small and beautiful business as ever-undulating rays of golden light which glistened and shone for all of us to bathe in. We were collecting accolades and praise like confetti. I couldn't have felt prouder. Following on from the Osborne visit, my office manager and I had been invited to No.10 Downing Street to attend a 'Small Business Think-Tank' day with a *Dragons' Den* star. It was like living in a dream... Local newspapers and TV stations often published the press releases I'd sent out highlighting the progress of our business, and my mind was set for the stars. 'Award-winning enterprise' and 'Life-affirming small business' the interviews and articles echoed. We were hurriedly hiring more and more staff. I felt unstoppable. It was the *best* feeling in the world. It was going stratospheric and there was *nothing* we couldn't do.....

But, was it? What had I missed? The outside world saw a very different image to that of our bookkeeper and accountant. We were young. Naive, foolish. Drunk with the first taste of success and I did not want to slow down. Not for anything. The ego loves this type of early success. I felt empowered, hungry, exhilarated and desperate for more but I was completely blind to the fact that we were spiralling into debt and collapse despite the whirlwind of success which was raging around us. My employees, unknowing of the fact that things were in fact deteriorating when the signs were all pointing to escalation, were urging me forward, keen for the right software, the appropriate machinery, for tools to be repaired, for vans to be serviced. Many were working overtime to keep up with the demand for orders, and the money was fast running out keeping up with it all.

I would spend my lunch breaks crying in my car. Phoning the business enterprise loan fund hotline, the crowdfunding agents, business advice lines, trying to find a way out. The bank wouldn't grant us an overdraft. The suppliers were sending bigger shipments and alongside these, bigger invoices. Invoices and Delivery Notes piled up on my desk. My employees wanted pay rises. My clients wanted discounts. The dark abyss swallowed me up. I sank down, and under ... and waited for the tidal wave to hit.

By Christmas I had let my entire workforce go. Every last one of them. With tears in my eyes. I explained, we just couldn't carry on. Just two weeks before Christmas. It was brutal. For them, especially. For me, even more so. I'd pushed so hard and driven the sales so much that I'd started to miss the glaringly obvious problems which had arisen in the fledgling business. With each new order, I was so buoyed by forward movement and dizzy with exhilaration that I'd failed to appreciate the value of slow, steady, well-managed growth and instead, had thrown everything we had at more, more, more. As a novice start-up entrepreneur, I'd failed to learn that it takes time and money to grow a business sustainably. You, my hesitant entrepreneur, may be likely to fall into the same trap – so, listen very carefully here. If you are a start-up, you likely won't have the cash reserves, the credit facilities, the contacts, the overdraft or the safety net which is available to more established enterprises. The feeling of growth is so intoxicating, and so thrilling that you, like a drug addict, will stop at nothing to obtain more. More staff. Bigger premises, more technology, more efficient processes, extra training, more equipment, hardware, software, machinery, vehicles ... the relentless demands of rapid growth are endless and quite unsustainable. Being a risk taker is an essential trait of an entrepreneur, but knowing when to put the brakes on or to say 'no' to an over-demanding client is a trait you must also cultivate.

The first few years of trading are particularly important. If your start-up is likely to collapse, it will be during those first three, difficult years. I had a product and a full order book. That's all you need, right? Wrong. I didn't have security. The profit margins were tight. My desire to please and eagerness to build everything for everyone, caused me to throw caution to the wind and we scaled up quickly. Too quickly. Growth is expensive. With each new contract or sale, you'll need the right level of staff. You need supplies, facilities, technical capabilities. What I hadn't written into the business model was the increase of overheads which follows on from the increase in orders. My prices remained more or less the same year after year and I worried about charging more (for all of us undervalue our product and services at the beginning) but my costs skyrocketed with every month that passed. And then, of course. There's the 'bad deal'. You will have one. I had over-promised and under-quoted for the largest project to date. A two-bed house – for a couple of farmers who wanted as much as possible for the lowest possible price. I was delighted to give discounts for such a prestigious order. Of course, the error was entirely mine. I was so eager to build it that I didn't care about the profit margin. I didn't realise how much a safety net was necessary and how out-of-budget my initial costing was. So, when the building was on site and clients were getting fidgety about delays and were piling more and more expectations onto my build team ... shit hit the fan. Big time. If a once-in-a-lifetime 'big deal' goes well, it can slingshot your business into stardom. If it goes wrong, you've expended all of your energy and workforce into one enormous contract which simply doesn't pay. My big deal crashed halfway through, and the largest invoice I'd ever issued for payment was never reconciled. Without an overdraft or savings to support such a substantial loss, the collapse was immediate.

I resisted it for a week or two. Stuck in denial and confusion. Furiously calculating strategies to mitigate the damage. Scribbling into my notepad late into the evening, most evenings, trying to figure out, to the nearest penny, how I could scrape by. Accepting that I had to close the business was the toughest call of my career. The hit to my ego plummeted it down to earth and I emerged again, more humble and more grounded than before. I had failed my first business. The initiation into entrepreneurship was complete.

Let's face it. One or more of your businesses will fail. People around you who will have been urging you to 'Play it safe' or have tried to be helpful by suggesting, 'Don't you think it's a bit risky?' or, 'Should you perhaps get a "real job"?' will be delighted that they have been proven right and will bask in their glory for some time. As awful as this is to bear, you can almost certainly convert this into motivational dynamite as you're peeling yourself back up again off the hard, cold bedrock you lie upon and slowly slide your trembling fingers back into those boxing gloves. Get. Back. Up.

I'm sure I don't need to tell you that a winner doesn't quit and a quitter never wins. You are in this *for life*. This is not a job, it's not a permanent fail. It's a hurdle. One down. If you've hit it and messed up, apologise, make amends, salvage what you can and then start running towards the next one. Jump higher this time. The experience will teach you more than instant success ever could. You'll better understand the rules of the game and be clear on the warning signs prior to an unfortunate event in the future. When I had problems with my first business, I literally crumbled. As I sat with an insolvency practitioner, new baby in my lap, in floods of tears and full of more self-doubt and conflict than I've ever felt in my life, he passed me a tissue and said, 'Listen. The only people I ever see in my office are business owners. Most "normal" people don't even make it to my office, they play it safe. They just don't risk it. They have comfortable jobs and they don't push for anything riskier than a mortgage. You at least tried.'

Thankfully I escaped without becoming bankrupt, but it was a close call. From that day on I promised to myself, I would go forth into the world and build something beautiful upon this experience. I had to start again, with a new business. I had little option but to partner with an investor who could help me start a commercial business which had the security my first enterprise lacked. Motivational leaders will tell ambitious first-time entrepreneurs to 'fall fast and fall hard' because the more you can practise the art of rising back up, the easier it will be to achieve success. A human toddler does not learn to walk without falling down. Often. You hop onto a bicycle and cycle around easily enough, for the falls and the scrapes when you were a kid enabled you to learn. A language cannot be mastered from one lesson, with a one phrase book. Get out there, make your mistakes. Go broke. Make money. Ride the tsunami of entrepreneurship and keep your mission in sight. There is nothing, just nothing, that can stop you, once you're on track.

And this leads me on to a few key principles of making your way into the world as a transformational female entrepreneur. Here are my most important pieces of advice for you.

Communication is key. In all the business screw-ups I've ever made, it's usually down to my lack of clarity with instructions or expectations or my inability to speak up honestly when something isn't right. Customers will all differ in their expectations of your company. Some will communicate well, and others will say nothing and give little feedback. If anything ever goes wrong and a customer is dissatisfied, the honest approach is far better than trying to blunder your way through excuses. My usual response if a customer is dissatisfied is, 'I am so sorry. Allow us to remedy this.' A fixed problem is not only a solution but it's excellent customer service. If you focus on customer service, above all else, you can't go far wrong. Maintain confidence, also, in yourself. It's sometimes difficult to speak up when five people want one thing and you feel, instinctively, that you need it to be another way. Women are wonderful at smoothing the conversation and being agreeable, but when it comes to your business, it needs your voice to be heard. Never shrink down and allow others to speak for you or over you when it was you who founded your own organisation. No matter how agreeable you wish to be. You've earned that right.

Practice gratitude. Of the best leaders I've come across, and from the research I've gathered on leadership, the most effective CEOs and entrepreneurs have worked tirelessly on their character. Mean-spirited people won't get far as an entrepreneur. If you practise gratitude, and feel thankful for your staff, your clients, associates and the opportunity you have, you will treat people accordingly. If you treat people well, and with kindness, they will (usually) respond with the same level of respect and treat you and your clients well in return.

Never borrow money from friends and family. When I was starting my first business, my friend and fellow college student joined me. She excitedly ploughed some of her savings into the business, which enabled us to build a showroom. Sadly, when the fledgling company collapsed, she had only managed to glean about half of what she invested back from the company and she lost a fair sum of money. Suffice it to say, we are no longer friends. It is worth thinking carefully about who you choose to bring into your start-up. I regret losing a friend. There is no guarantee with business, and if you wish to keep your friends and family, please don't borrow from them. You may lose a lot more than money.

Do your due diligence. I didn't honestly appreciate the value of this advice until very recently. As a positive 'glass half-full' kind of girl, I was often welcoming anyone into my organisation with open arms. Delighted in the positively helpful and charming individuals who gracefully glided into the organisation as partners, investors, directors and mentors. Not once did I think to run a background check. Beware ... there are predators.

BEWARE! PREDATORS...

Every business is about understanding people. Which people you have to get through. Which people you have to embrace. Which people you have to jump over. Which people you have to push out of the way. That's the game.

Donny Deutsch

There is one huge flaw in the character of many idealistic start-up entrepreneurs. We are aspirational beings, hard-wired to look for the positives and seek out opportunities; this can compromise our ability to recognise red flags. (Plus, we don't give in easily, not when we've poured so much of our heart into our enterprise.) With this being said, it's absolutely imperative that you learn as much as you can about people. Research psychology and read *The 48 Laws of Power* by Robert Greene.

I believe most people are inherently good. Until, that is, you ascend up the ladder into commercial business and, then, into a boardroom. There, you will find a demographic of people quite unlike those you've encountered before. If you, like me, aren't familiar with predatory behaviour, it will likely be a shock to you when you encounter it for the first time. The problem with deceit and malpractice is that it's usually executed in such a way as to be wholly unthinkable to you. If you can't imagine it, how could you possibly look for it? I honestly had no idea that once I became a business owner, I'd need to defend myself from the myriad of highly skilled sharks who circle hungrily around small and growing businesses. These folks simply devour inexperienced entrepreneurs.

We are like juicy little whitebait to them. The very worst type (as far as I understand it), weave an impeccably crafted invisibility cloak around themselves. This is the false persona: a character. Then they identify your weaknesses, play up to your aspirations, earn your trust and quietly gather their equally devious cartel around them. They then patiently wait for the perfect time to strike. It could be months, years or decades before they fully execute their plan.

The sharks aren't easy to identify; they come with smiling faces and warm hands. They are motivated by one thing only. Accessing your money. They will lie, cheat and charm you into thinking that they're the best asset you have. Therefore, to be a successful business owner, you'll need to understand who's actually on your team and who is in fact a smiling assassin, waiting for you to drop your guard and strip you bare.

Sadly, it's not just investors, partners or advisors who you need to watch. Money and power can, and does corrupt your most trusted employees.

Dacher Keltner writes for the *Harvard Review* about 'The Paradox of Power'. It's entirely plausible that you could hire a perfectly good employee, only to promote them years later to an executive or director. Once they are in a position of power, they transition from a 'good employee' to your very worst nightmare.

'A paradox of power' is that people gain their power through virtuous behaviours such as collaboration, openness, fairness and sharing, but once they enjoy a position of privilege, those finer qualities start to fade. Research shows that the powerful are more likely to engage in rude, selfish, and unethical behaviour.

Studies show that people in positions of corporate power are three times as likely as those at the lower rungs of the ladder to interrupt co-workers, multitask during meetings, raise their voices, and say insulting things at the office. And people who've just moved into senior roles are particularly vulnerable to losing their virtues. The nineteenth century historian and politician Lord Acton got it right: Power *does* tend to corrupt.

The consequences can be far-reaching. The abuse of power ultimately tarnishes the reputations of executives, undermining their opportunities for influence. It also creates stress and anxiety among their colleagues, diminishing productivity and creativity in the group and dragging down team members' engagement and performance. In a recent poll of 800 managers and employees in seventeen industries, about half the respondents who reported being treated rudely at work said they deliberately decreased their effort or lowered the quality of their work in response.

So, as you build your first enterprise, recognise that you first need to understand psychology. Give someone too much power? They will quickly undermine you and undo a lot of your hard work, all the while seeking to claim your place as the leader. I would recommend you read *Snakes in Suits* by Paul Babiak, PhD and Robert D. Hare, PhD before scaling an organisation or partnering with anyone, to fully understand how predatory behaviour manifests in a business and corporate setting.

You see, many social predators may lack the ability to perceive or care how their behaviour affects others, leading them to break promises, reveal private information, and take credit for others' accomplishments. They get away with it by being perfect chameleons, ingratiating themselves in an often drawn-out dance with victims (you!) that targets their ego and unique vulnerabilities. You, dear reader, will be vulnerable in the early days of your first successful enterprise.

Fortunately, I have learnt the most difficult lesson on your behalf; so I can relay this to you, and save you the pain. You see, my next business was completely different. It actually scaled far further than the first and reached over £1m in revenue which was a dream come true for me. But, this came at a hefty price.

Unfortunately I recognised far too late into the latest enterprise that I was embroiled in someone else's power game. One which I was too exhausted to play and too naive to fully appreciate. So, I just quietened my voice, focused on what I enjoyed in the business and let it run its course. I loved my clients and, as such, I was often away on long business trips. It was therefore essential that I had partners in the business who could manage the day-to-day operations. I quelled my suspicions, for the business I'd dreamed of for so many years was real, it was growing, it was beautiful. This is what I'd dreamed of. I convinced myself that I was merely paranoid and chose to ignore the knowing glances between co-directors who seemed to know a lot more than I did about the operations and the bank statements. I chose to ignore the nagging feeling that things weren't right. Besides, I was utterly locked in, both emotionally and financially. After so many years of being a start-up founder, I was finally generating a good salary for myself. Besides, with young children to support I couldn't quit my own business; and it was clear that the other directors weren't intending to go anywhere, either. A friend of mine did a background check on one of my business partners. A self-proclaimed multi-millionaire business person. It transpired that this person was a ghost. No track record of any business success, not a single mention of this person anywhere online. No historical records. No newspaper articles. As if they'd never existed. Not even a Linkedin account or Facebook page. Nothing. 'This person is a complete nobody!!!' my friend exclaimed in horror. I shrugged. It's OK, I reassured him. They're just old school. Denial, Denial, Denial.

I clenched my teeth and pushed ahead. It was about five years later that I deeply regretted not taking action sooner. My business partner had fired all of my original staff members and instead hired personal friends. Then he convinced me that it was essential to coordinate a round of funding, from investors with no background in business and brought no value whatsoever (apart from complicating the decision-making process), and if we didn't we'd go bankrupt. Rather than check the figures for myself, I trusted him blindly. My shareholding was now down to less than 33%. He chose to use his own accountants who were close friends and decided to keep the banking transactions and accounting under lock and key. I was told, repeatedly, to 'keep my nose out' and trust that it's all under control. Sales and Marketing was my department. Accounts and Operations was theirs. I was busy building the brand. So, I focused on that. As an optimist, I was utterly convinced that the business, now trading at £1.3m year on year was destined to be a £5m company soon enough. I could just wait it out, surely?

But waiting it out wasn't easy. I was soon demoted to a small voice on an impossibly large board of shareholders, only one of which was my friend and ally, Dawn. The board was quite obviously corrupted and, like a disease, darkness spread across the organisation. Dawn texted me one evening, after a particularly awkward and frustrating board meeting to offer support. 'Gemma,' it read, 'I'm worried about you. Please, speak to my advisor, find a way to sell it, and get out.'

With that, she passed me the number of a trusted contact of hers. I needed to exit, and rapidly. I started to worry. Huge problems started to materialise. I started to notice the numbers weren't stacking up. Profits were dropping out of the organisation, money was being siphoned off somewhere. The investment, (a figure in excess of one hundred thousand pounds) seemingly disappeared into thin air after hitting the current account and then vanishing into a savings account which was, quite conveniently, closed down soon after. I only discovered this fact years later when running my own unofficial audit.

Being on the road a lot, I was often very busy, so I had little choice but to trust that my company co-directors had it under control. Things started to look very bleak when the accountants became defensive and were refusing to audit the accounts. To make matters worse, clients were being mistreated by a very inexperienced and newly appointed director who was far from qualified for the position and was making obscene errors. Mistakes which I couldn't remedy. Without the shareholders support, I couldn't fire the individual, no matter how much evidence I brought forward. Then I realised that the shareholders were not there to bring funding (that, of course, had disappeared) but were instead a key component of the now firmly entrenched power game. Their presence diminished mine even further. Now a minority shareholder, I had, quite literally, given my voice away to others who quite frankly, didn't care about any of the values which I had founded the entire business on. They were just observers, who happened to have taken control of the ship.

The ship had run aground. But there was no room left for me at the wheel.

At a time when the business needed my leadership more than ever, I was unable to effect the slightest bit of change. I demanded shareholder meeting after shareholder meeting. I made a report, took notes, sent emails, ran an investigation, reported my findings to the shareholders, consulted solicitors and advisors, called the clients and listened to their problems, relayed those problems and requested that we restructure the organisation. I had aspirations of hiring a competent director, and getting this business back in shape. Amazingly, the shareholders remained completely silent. It was quite bizarre. Either nobody cared, or they were all in on it. I couldn't figure out which was which. I was perplexed that these people didn't actually want to remedy the problems, and instead, wanted to remain in control yet knowing they were slowly suffocating the organisation by their inaction. Quite simply, the business had been hijacked, and there was absolutely nothing I could do about it.

After a lengthy process of undertaking several months worth of due diligence on the executive team, I realised that I'd been well and truly hoodwinked. But, there was one final blow of the axe which had yet to fall.

In the midst of this terrifying investigation, and on the 11 February 2022, newspaper headlines declared that '"Secret Millionaire" Dawn dies after 30 years of business brilliance'.

I had been waiting for the call. I knew it was coming, for she'd been courageously living with stage four stomach cancer for twelve months, but was heartbroken that it happened so quickly. Dawn was a proven business woman with a very public track record. Not only a remarkable businesswoman but a former 'secret millionaire' who helped to transform the construction and manufacturing industries. Over the years, Dawn had proven her worth as an entrepreneur, and clocked up a number of prestigious awards including the 'Most Influential Person in British Manufacturing', 'Pioneer of the Life of Our Nation' and 'Veuve Clicquot Business Woman of the Year', as well as three honorary doctorates from the universities of Staffordshire, Manchester and Chester.

On Linkedin, a statement from her enterprise, the now international Flowcrete, said: 'It is with deep sadness the Flowcrete family laments the death of our matriarch and co-founder, Dr Dawn Gibbins, MBE. Dawn is in our eyes one of the greatest business women this nation has ever produced, setting an example at a very young age to other women in construction.'

That's when I knew, that the last shining light of leadership had been extinguished. It was on my forty-second birthday, in the midst of uncovering the scale of misconduct in my executive team, that I recognised that the ride was over. Dawn has always phoned me on my birthday, and remained, throughout the entirety of my start-up journey, the rock that supported me on the journey as a founder. The lights went out. Leaving us on my birthday was especially profound. I emailed my resignation to the shareholders. I gave up the fight. It was over.

Needless to say, my departure gave those who remained the opportunity to take the rest for themselves. The business was stripped of any cash and assets that had remained. They disappeared off with the value of my entire life's work. Selling off all of the company assets, including the website I'd built from scratch when Esmee was a baby, everything was transferred into another entity with a similar company name. Wriggling through every little loophole, squeezing any last ounce of goodness out of that beautiful business and taking what they could for themselves. And I, the designer and founder, cast adrift, with my best clients equally stunned beside me. Without Dawn, that business has now run its course. The most heartbreaking ending, to the most aspirational and inspirational business.

The reason I am sharing this story, dear reader, is not to put you off your adventure or scare you into never taking the steps into entrepreneurship but to give you a full and honest account of the risks you take when your time comes. As your business grows, so must you. Rather than being a start-up founder and grateful for every opportunity and desperate for sales, you must become a business person instead. More logical, pragmatic and cautious. Slow down. Don't accept investment from anyone you've not run a background check on. Obtain character references, ask for evidence of previous business trading history. Seek references from their previous companies. Spend time with them, for months, years, before giving them shares.

As with any personal relationship, a business relationship can still be an abusive relationship. The most skilled fraudsters will have been destroying other people's livelihoods for their entire careers so they are exceptionally talented at it.

Things to look out for in this regard are:

- Do your new executives or partners make claims to have built their own wildly successful businesses? (Check Companies House – do not simply take their word for it.)

- Do they get defensive if you ask for proof and do you feel awkward asking?

- Do the new executives, shareholders or directors have genuine references? (Other than their mates.)

- Are these individuals bringing in their own accountants, friends or investors with them as part of the deal? If so, they will most likely be planning to overpower your executive team and coordinate a siege.

- Does anyone you are working with, or seeking to invest, show signs of having a controlling personality? Do they lack empathy? Will they seek to belittle you or a member of staff for their own kicks?

If you have answered yes to any of these questions, engage with a solicitor as soon as you possibly can and find a way to extract them from your organisation; or at the very least, retain 51% of the shareholding and seek a way to buy them out.

If you aren't already committed, find a way to release your connection to this person and start again. You can set up again either alone or with the right person. You will always be you, the innovator, the creator. Focus your creative skills on an enterprise which will support you and your family for the rest of your lives, not one which will become a source of upset, distress and misery. Above all else, don't put too much emphasis on shareholders' agreements and non-disclosure agreements. Legal paperwork is a good deterrent but unless you have a huge amount of capital behind you to afford hefty lawyers' fees, the process of enforcing these terms is practically impossible. Companies House Act 2006 has very clear legislation on what directors can and can't do in a limited company. This is reassuring and comforting when you're dealing with individuals who are breaking the law on multiple counts.

Sadly, when striving to expose malpractice or corruption, Companies House does not enforce this legislation. However, one regulatory body, the Insolvency Service does have the power to investigate and strike off directors who are breaking the law, but unfortunately are very resistant to investigating directors' or companies' unless there is an extreme circumstance and it's putting the public at risk. Suffice it to say, when things go wrong, irrespective of whether the law is on your side or not, you're largely on your own. It would be worth taking out a legal insurance package or setting some savings aside for legal matters should they arise in the future. Forewarned is forearmed!

MONEY, MONEY, MONEY...

Money often costs too much.

Ralph Waldo Emerson

Several months ago, a friend of mine who was looking to leave her job to start her own consultancy business came to me for reassurance. She wanted to understand how she wasn't going to lose out financially should she take the leap. 'How am I going to be able to earn the same salary as I am now?' she implored, anxiously struggling to figure out how she would make ends meet. A heavy, expectant silence hung on the end of the telephone whilst she nervously awaited my response. Most likely, she had imagined I'd have a quick and witty response which would magically solve this problem. Something about Venture Capitalists, Start-up Grants or magic money trees for those of us who are brave enough to reach out for them. But sadly, after considering this for a few moments, I had no choice but to be honest. 'You won't,' I replied.

It's a conundrum we all face when stepping out into the world, alone and without a boss to ensure our pay cheque is issued each month. The psychology behind money is always going to be difficult for many first-time entrepreneurs. Rather than give my own interpretation of the 'whys' and 'hows', I figured it was best to interview the expert on freedom and anarchy, Tom Hodgkinson.

Tom Hodgkinson is a British writer and the editor of *The Idler* magazine, which he established in 1993. His philosophy, in his published books and articles, is of a relaxed approach to life, enjoying it as it comes rather than toiling for an imagined better future.

Back in 1991, bored to tears by his job, 23-year-old journalist Tom Hodgkinson lay on his bed and dreamed of starting a magazine called *The Idler*. He'd found the title in a collection of essays by Dr Johnson, himself a constitutionally indolent man. How to live, that was the question. How to be free in a world of jobs and debt? And curse this alarm clock.

Tom was fortunately sacked from his job and started to sign on. He wandered across the road to where his old friend, designer and writer Gavin Pretor-Pinney lived. Gavin was the kind of person who could help Tom to realise this dream. And he did. In August 1993, the pair produced issue one of *The Idler*. It had the subtitle, 'Literature for loafers'. Dr Johnson was the cover star and there was an interview with magic mushroom guru Terence McKenna. Contributors included a young journalist called Louis Theroux.

His books *Business for Bohemians* (2017) and *The Idler's Manual* (2021) are certainly worth a read.

Tom has summarised for you why he thinks you should quit your job.

'Having control of your own time is absolutely brilliant. It's important to recognise that leaving a corporate job and starting your own business brings you a level of freedom. But you must, of course, be mindful of the type of business you create. You may end up creating something riddled with problems, but at least the problems will be *yours!* I think, for certain people, it's extremely stressful being employed. It's not fun. It's boring and laborious, and it depends much on whether you have a good manager, etc. It's not even that secure, you could be made redundant, and you're always under threat of being fired, so it's not really worthwhile if you're not enjoying it. Friends of mine, in corporate jobs, are always under threat of being sacked and if you do keep your job, you're in the climate of fear anyway, which isn't a great place to be.

'You need to realise that you can live on much less money than you are earning in your full-time job. In fact, I don't think many people realise that they are not going to *need* to create the same level of income by freelancing. Your costs are going to diminish immediately, once you've left your job. In everyday life, you don't need to spend as much as you think you do. I've worked out that, overnight (by leaving your job) you are immediately saving over £10,000 per year. *Having a job is very expensive*. Let's look at it this way: you're losing money through the amount you pay in taxes, in commuting, coffees, sandwiches, work suits. Think about how much you're spending on lunches for example – just £5 or £6 per day could be as much as £1,500 per year. What else could you be doing with that money? You've got to start by being frugal. You can't expect to live at the same level of luxury as you perhaps were previously. You've got to think of simple things like getting rid of the car. (We just buy old bangers instead, and cycle everywhere).

One amazing benefit, I've personally found, is that we don't need to buy as many new clothes. Without travelling into an office every day, you can just wear the same clothes you would at home. In addition, you're not spending £20-30 on the pub after work with your work colleagues. Another interesting observation of leaving a job you don't particularly enjoy, is that you don't have to spend money on all of those 'little treats', which you buy yourself because you feel you deserve it. It all adds up, you know?

My advice to anyone looking to quit their job is this: Just sit down with a spreadsheet and work out the costs of the job. Think about how much your job is costing you. Nobody ever thinks of this. When you've left, you don't have to pay such a high level of income tax and national insurance and you might not pay any tax at all if you're not making a profit initially.

So many people work in careers because they like the job title and the backdrop of the organisation behind them. But my perspective is, you could be earning half what you are now and you'd be much happier. You won't need the expensive holidays if your mental health is in a good place, for your life will be happier. For example, I enjoy the freedom of playing sport after lunch, and being in control of my life is quite exhilarating. The downsides: I realised that when we had a bookshop – managing staff, paying rent, and by the end we were paying ourselves £0 which was a total nightmare. So, we gave that up and we were doing Airbnb to make ends meet, renting out our children's bedrooms which wasn't always ideal. In truth, there have been some really awful times! The children didn't always appreciate the value of being poor! But the upsides and the freedom it allowed us more than compensated for this. This really does depend on your life circumstances and whether you have young children but if you are in a position when you cannot stand your job for a moment longer, that is really bad news for your mental health. That affects your whole family. The upside of self-employment is that you have far more time at home – this can benefit your family. What's important to you?

Not having a job can be incredibly liberating. You can find that space where you can just be who you are. The people who are in newspapers, politicians, people who run big corporations etc., all have these big stupid titles. I mean, what's it all for? Titles can be helpful but I don't think we should identify ourselves through the job title which is given us. When I was at *The Guardian*, we were offered quite high-up jobs in the company after launching *The Idler* and we were brought back on board but we made a point that we didn't actually want job titles. In fact, we weren't really interested in working for the newspapers. We didn't like the office politics. It was short-lived. I left and I haven't had a 'job' since 1997. I find this suits me perfectly.

One warning I suppose. You are going to reach a point in your mid-fifties where your friends who stuck out at jobs from their twenties are now earning enormous sums of money and have quietly worked up the ranks in their boring professions. It's hard for someone like myself to see these people who stuck at their jobs doing really well financially decades later. Just turning up every day – can pay off financially. When you see them sending their children to private schools, living in their big houses… it can make you doubt your choices. But, you have to be strong. I value my mental health and my freedom too much to jeopardise that for wealth. If you're miserable in your job but you stick with it purely for the money? What does this say about you? This, I suppose is where morality comes in. Some people will value money over friendships and family. If you ultimately value work and money over your family and friends, you could end up losing the very things that are important to you. Philosophically, I believe, walking away from all of this… it's the key to the good life. It can just be so powerful. But when you see your neighbour buy their Tesla, you need to appreciate that you might also want one or you may feel resentful for not pushing for the big expensive things others have. But the neighbour with the Tesla might yearn for a yacht. The desire for more just never ends. Philosophers will often cite that you should be happy with no money. But Aristotle, and others, have suggested that a reasonable amount of money should make you happy. There needs to be a middle ground. The middle state is the one to aim for. Either end of that spectrum, too little money, or too much money, can cause so many problems. The work that I do rewards me with enough but in addition, there's something other than the money. I love the feedback I receive from readers and I am always inspired by other people. I'm inspired by the Greek philosophers and it's always been there. I look back at my diary from my 18-year-old self, and I am happy to report that I am exactly the same person that I always have been.

And of course, there's the incredible amount of time you'll now have. It's an amazing luxury to feel like I've got all the time in the world. I have learnt to desire less and enjoy more. The little things that I like are always so easy to get. I suppose I would encourage you to look into philosophy. I personally lean towards Epicureanism. It is a philosophy based on the teachings of Epicurus. Epicureanism is a form of hedonism, which declares that pleasure is the only good there is. Epicureanism says that the absence of pain is the greatest pleasure; it also advocates a simple life. If a job is painful to you, you are better off seeking that which gives you pleasure. It is worth immersing yourself in philosophy to really cultivate your mental strength to resist the trappings of the employment system. Just read as much as you can. I was reading Plato last night and I need to keep on top of reading and continue to do so simply to remind myself of what makes a 'good life'.

It boils down to this really. You just don't have to be rich to have a good lifestyle. I like beer and bacon. If I can be really honest with myself, what do I need to make myself happy? I can lie in. I can wake up late. I don't need to be in the office until 11 a.m. I can play tennis after lunch. The successful person gets to do what they *really want to do.* If you can turn the 'stuff you like to do' into a profession that pays – this is the highest way of life. You may feel that you are not creative, I would argue that you are.

Think carefully about this. Who are you? What are you suited for? What does your personality lend itself to? If you get your priorities in the right place, and work with your skills to find a way to make money from what you are inherently good at, do that.'

Creating business is so vitally important. Not just for those you serve, but to enable you to really drill down into what you want from your time and how you might go about living your best life. Tom speaks authentically about not wanting to be tied down to a job – his work and his philosophy continue to inspire others who are also seeking a more anarchistic way of life. If you are reading this book, and you have made it this far, I am nothing short of convinced that you already know that your current situation isn't 'freedom' for you. If you need any further philosophical advice on this topic – seek out Alan Watts. He was a guiding light for me in the early days.

Deep down, despite the money concerns, you know that freedom lies just outside of these pages. Freedom to be who you are is woven into the business you are soon to create. The mere act of accepting that money will not flow to a start-up but must be earned, penny by penny. Your job is to work through your idea. Get it down on paper. Research it. Develop it and then get out there and try it. If it's too difficult for you to quit your job immediately, try to go part-time. Narrow your hours down by a day or two a week to allow you the breathing space to develop your idea and become accustomed to the lower level of income. You can of course research grants and funding but you'll need (a) a watertight plan and projections and (b) to understand you could lose shares and control of your business and (c) you'll be more successful obtaining grants if you are a 'not-for-profit'.

What are you currently spending money on which you could drop from your life today? Do you have savings or assets you could utilise to carry you through the first six to twelve months? I sold my car when I was developing my first business. In addition (which I do not encourage you to do) I used my credit cards to purchase household goods. I stopped going out. I cooked more. The expensive hobbies were dropped. Ask yourself this one question: 'Is the rest of my life important to me?' Are you sacrificing your time for money which you might be able to cope without?

My journey has taken a decade. I'm sorry to report that I didn't have an actual salary for the first couple of years. I believed that it was more important to pay my staff first and get the business well and truly off the ground. This may not suit you, and you should probably decide to start a business which can pay you a basic salary from the very first order.

You will soon be able to justify a great salary as the founder and executive of your own company and hold the shareholding of a business which is worth infinitely more than your salary. This is true freedom, my hesitant entrepreneur. No restrictions. No fear. All you need to do, is recognise that this comes at a cost. Less money for a small period of time. The temporary discomfort of making the transition. But, that's a very worthwhile investment into the rest of your life – isn't it?

NB: You might be able to design your salary into the business model from day one but you might have to drop your salary expectations. My friend at the Whaley Bridge Canal Group is earning a good salary from selling books and running markets. If you are happy to start small, you could start by applying for grants and investments or find a business coach who can help you set something up quickly so you can take a salary out of the first few months' revenue. Your journey is likely to be significantly easier than mine. I took the difficult path. You may not need to.

BECOME AN ENTREPRENEUR WHILE STILL EMPLOYED

I pretended to be somebody I wanted to be, until I finally became that person. Or he became me.

Cary Grant

(formerly Archie Leech)

The statement 'quit your job' is not only practically impossible and wildly insensitive but probably the most irritating suggestion anyone can give you at this moment in time. If it were that easy, wouldn't you have done it already? For many of you reading this book, the distance between 'here' and 'there' is such an enormous chasm that you are already irritated at the mere suggestion of it. If you have children, it's also possible that the idea of running away from your career to a new start-up with no money and no security would be downright irresponsible and would put their lives under unnecessary strain. Why would any self-respecting adult or parent willingly put themselves in such a ridiculous situation? It's madness. Insanity. Ludicrous. Yes. Yes, all of these statements are true and I do not wish to irritate you further by labouring the point.

There is another way.

The way to be an entrepreneur is to seek out opportunities and build a career for yourself, right? This is because you want to enjoy your work? Right? Do you think that perhaps you already have a solution sitting right under your nose? Perhaps freedom comes not from running away, but from running *towards* your employer and the business for which you work? Now, I shall explain how someone might actually get to have both. Employment and entrepreneurship! The next story could illustrate how you could build a new career for yourself ... through your current job.

Depending on the size and complexity of the organisation you work for, you may be presented with a range of different opportunities. Let me give you an example.

Bob works for an industrial machine manufacturer called Pro-Bel. They produce all manner of machinery as production line equipment for food manufacturers. Being an engineering firm, this company is run and managed primarily by engineers and is highly technical. The engineers at director level have exceptional technical ability and are consistently working on the best output rates of their machines. Two of their best sellers are the AP89 and the A129 models. High performance, linear conveyor packing machines, specifically designed to reduce labour costs involved with packaging sandwiches into cardboard sleeves. They can pack an astonishing 45 sandwiches a minute! These glistening stainless steel powerhouses are at the high end of the market and their digital display panels and button interfaces evoke the image of an Airbus A300 flight deck. At six-foot high, two-metres wide and running the length of a football pitch, they are the crème de la crème of the food production industry technology systems.

Bob has a very love/hate relationship with his career at Pro-Bel. He is an engineer. His father was an engineer, as was his grandfather. His job was predestined. He loves the company he works for and takes pride in the machines he works on. Bob is well liked by his peers and his boss and he is earning an excellent salary with the usual perks a successful employee gains from a secure job. His three children are now at secondary school and his life is coasting along really well. He's 'almost' content. The drive to work is only a fifteen minute journey from his beautiful semi-detached home in Bracknell, Reading. The factory is on an industrial estate in a place called Lower Earley. It's flanked by long sweeping lawns and trees. The work environment is as you'd expect for a large, successful engineering firm. Long, zinc-clad industrial units with a large floor to ceiling glass entrance lobby. Through the glass entrance doors, the lobby presents sweeping curved reception desks, comfortable sofas and the entrance to a large staff canteen peppered with cheerful co-workers. Not a bad place to be. Over the past few years though, Bob has been feeling restless. He is working in the job he *should* be happy with. It's not the job that's getting him down. He thinks that the problem lies with the factory. He feels as though he's not progressing.

Bob is a man who loves to be outdoors. Whenever Bob is out and about in his town, he's the chap who stops to speak to everyone he knows and he's always helping his neighbours and friends. Bob loves listening to problems and giving friendly advice. He sees himself as a friendly and helpful person and when he's engaging with others it lights him up. After spending eight years travelling to and from the factory as a full-time employee he's wondering whether he should really be there. He's picked up several business start-up books and dreams of one day setting up his own business. Given that he's an engineer and he loves helping people, he's decided to set up a local repair shop. This would give him both the interaction and the freedom he so desperately seeks. But, being hesitant about stepping away from his career to develop his own business he decides to see whether he has the skills to spot opportunities and establish himself as a creative entrepreneur. Are engineers creative? He feels as though he is, but he simply knows nothing about business. Where would he even begin to start? His wife jokes that he's having a midlife crisis and his children are starting to wonder when the sports car will arrive on the driveway. Rather than give in to his dreams and set up his shop, he decides instead to experiment with the current job. What if he can be an entrepreneur from within Pro-Bel? Could he find a project to side-step into? Could he find a way to create the lifestyle he'd like without having to leave his job?

Bob is reclining back on a patio chair on an unusually warm spring evening with his friend and neighbour, Mike. Mike reaches over and passes him a cold beer. 'Hey!' he exclaims, 'how's it going over there at Pro-Bel?' Bob distractedly runs his thumb along the condensation on the label. He slides one fingernail under the corner, dislodging the fragile paper and starts to tear it from the glass. Bob grimaces and opens up with a joke about quitting his job to find freedom from the monotony of a nine to five. Rolling his eyes for effect, he leans back and chuckles at his predicament. Mike is an excellent listener who loves nothing more than a lively debate; so he probes further, trying to understand the nature of the situation and help his friend seek a solution. Bob explains that he's not yet ready to 'Go it alone' and that he wants to create a new business for himself whilst still remaining employed. 'There must be a way I can prove to myself that I have the skills to be entrepreneurial,' he muses whilst he takes a sip of his beer and surveys the garden around them, enjoying the incoming dusk as the sky darkens and streaks with purples, pinks and reds. Mike agrees with him and recommends that he starts by looking at the company as a whole and downloading the filed accounts from Companies House. Mike is an accountant, so from his perspective, everything starts and ends with the company accounts. 'This,' he proclaims, 'is the window through which to view the company,' to understand it's current position. Every limited company operating in the UK must file their accounts annually and they are visible to members of the public. So, Mike rushes into the house, brings out his laptop and chuckles as he places it on the patio table between them. 'Government website – Companies House!' he exclaims proudly, as he taps it into Google, finds the website and types in the company name, 'Pro-Bel Ltd'.

Together, they scroll down through a historical list of every year's trading history. Bob doesn't yet understand how to read a 'Profit and Loss' or a 'Balance Sheet' so Mike shows him that the company is bringing in an enormous amount of money (revenue) but isn't making a profit. The profit figure, at the end of the balance sheet shows the figure in brackets. When you see a figure, indicated like this – '(£80,000.00)' – rather than – '£80,000.00' – it means that the money is actually a loss. Not a gain. Mike suggested that the company may need a bit of an entrepreneurial boost, for their sake, rather than his. If it's not making money, how secure is his job?

However, the company had a substantial amount of stock, machinery, vans and commercial buildings (assets). So this, as far as Mike could see, was positive for the company. Many companies trundle along for years without making significant profits especially if they have borrowed capital (in Pro-Bel's case, to invest in the machinery and the factory) and it's highly probable that a company showing small but consistent loss has not yet recovered from the investment that it had to make in setting up their factory. Despite this, making losses, year after year, in the long term is never a particularly good sign, so clearly there was a change which needed to take place at Pro-Bel. What Bob also noticed was that the revenue was high but the amount of money in the bank account, 'cash in bank and in hand', was low. This could indicate a cash flow issue. He knows that the machines are very expensive. Pro-Bel may only sell ten of their machines a year. But at half a million pounds per piece, that's not bad going! However, have you ever heard of the phrase, 'Don't put all of your eggs in one basket'? What if one of these machines went without payment or their customer went into administration? Just one order like this makes up over six weeks of production time which would present a big problem for any company. Bob thanked his neighbour and resolved to think long and hard about what he could take from this and how he might be able to help.

A week or so later, Bob bit the bullet. He needed advice. So, after searching 'free business support' on Google he found a government website called Business Growth Hub which helps businesses grow. When he explained what he was trying to achieve, and that he wanted to find a way to identify where his company/employer may be making a loss and how he could assist them with turning it around, he was allocated a wonderful mentor called Gillian who spent an hour with him on the phone, every other Tuesday morning. Wow, what a wonderful experience it was, for him to be able to ask questions about profits, trading history, price points and market demand, with someone who knew what they were talking about, and learn about the mechanisms of business.

Bob was thrilled to recognise that a business works a little like a machine. The cogs and the dials, the input and the output. The software (processes) and the hardware (products). He could understand that his job was a small part of a complex machine which runs on an external factor (market demand)

and operates through different mechanisms (departments) to produce an end result (profit). What he also recognised was that his problem-solving skills weren't just limited to the machinery he worked on.

He could, for an hour a day, shift his focus to the main problem he wanted to solve for his boss.

The profit. So, the market demand was driving the sales of the machinery. But, who were those clients? What was it they were investing in?

They were:
commercial food producers
wishing to minimise labour costs
seeking to improve efficiency.

Bob had a chat to his business mentor who suggested that he look at analysing a typical client and identify *what else* they were buying. She also suggested that he look at whether he could find a way to improve Pro-Bel's current offering. Are there any upgrades or bolt-ons that could improve their cash flow? Perhaps lower-priced items in numerous amounts of multiple orders? But Bob couldn't even comprehend making a cheap machine. That was unthinkable. What else was there?

Over many weeks, Bob set about his task as if he were designing his own business. He spent many of his evenings researching the target market, products within the market sector he operated in, and looking with fresh eyes at typical clients and Pro-Bel's competitors. He felt like a private investigator! What a thrill it was to be outside of his comfort zone! He worked out how to write a business plan. Yes, it was in his free time. But this was, in his mind, the equivalent to doing a business course and he was learning new skills, so rather than resent spending the time, he looked forward to it.

The 'AHA!!!' moment came to him a few months after embarking on his clandestine project.

He drew up a report of his findings (but gracefully omitted the part about his research on the companies accounts!!). With help from Mike he worked out a 'revenue projection' of how much money they could make from his idea and then broke this down to how much profit the company might be able to make over the next five years. He made phone calls to suppliers and drew up a spreadsheet of costs which would be incurred to make such a change. Then he obtained price lists from the other companies selling the same products he was hoping to sell. But, would the clients buy his idea? 'I'd best check!!' he declared to himself as he scanned the Pro-Bel customer database and picked up the phone. After contacting a dozen of their existing clients, he felt more convinced than ever that he was onto something. As he ran the idea by them, they all responded positively and all but one asked him for a price list.

Then, one bright, sunny morning in mid-June he woke with a clear sense of resolution. His research was complete. He was ready to test it. He padded into his office and printed his report. He drove straight to the local printers on the way into the factory and had it wire bound (this was an important document to both him and to Pro-Bel). Walking into the foyer, with the professional Business Plan under his arm, he made a beeline directly to his boss's office.

Within a few weeks of the conversation with his boss, his business plan made its journey through the upper executive team, passing through the scrutiny of the directors and up to the shareholders. The report was taken positively, and Bob had in fact correctly identified that the company could make an additional line of products which would complement the range of machines, without disrupting Pro-Bel's current manufacturing processes.

The packaging components to go with the machines!

He calculated that if their machines were packing 45 sandwiches a minute, the clients must also have a purchasing budget for the packaging! Some of his existing clients were kind enough to explain to him over the phone what their average spend was and what quantities they usually bought. He gathered information on film trays, sandwich boards, polystyrene trays and cardboard tubs. These supplies had an extremely fast turnaround and were small but consistent orders which would bring Pro-Bel the cash flow it needed to support the more complex, long-term, large machine orders. Given that the food manufacturers have a clear objective to improve efficiency and reduce labour costs – why not save them the job of ordering the supplies from one company and the machine from another? Why not just bundle the two together and have one core supplier? It made sense to the clients and it made sense to their accountants.

So. A new line was born. Bob was sent out on numerous assignments to visit the food packaging companies they were sourcing their stock from and developing new sealing methods for their machines. Bob, supported by his boss, developed a completely new packaging material and sealing process. This was an 'eco' product and was the UK's first, fully gas-tight cardboard tray which had a heat-sealed, transparent film lid. This product was only possible through the technology provided by the Pro-Bel machine, so their clients had exclusive access to it. That, of course, drove more clients to purchase the Pro-Bel machine over their competitors. The competitors simply couldn't match this offering.

Following on from this turn of events, Bob realised that he did, in fact, have the creativity required to become an entrepreneur. There are an infinite amount of possibilities for the conclusion of this story but I'll give you three scenarios to give you an idea of how this could work out.

Scenario one: Armed with new-found knowledge and having gained the experience necessary to identify a need and present a solution, Bob decided to set up a repair shop. But, this time, he spent twice as long on his business plan as he did on the Pro-Bel plan and developed, not just a local repair shop, but a national one. He resigned from Pro-Bel and developed an online repairs firm which worked with couriers to collect and deliver all manner of small electrical items like radios and coffee machines, and returned them back after repair at his national depot, not far from the factory, in Reading. The shareholders of Pro-Bel were keen to assist him with his venture and they provided a small amount of seed fund investment capital to secure his repair depot tenancy and purchase some equipment. The Pro-Bel shareholders hold 10% of the equity in his new start-up and he's now working with them to develop a subsidiary packaging plant based in the north of England.

Scenario two: The kudos this project gave him was immense; Bob was not only congratulated and welcomed to join the board of directors but he was also free to dictate his own schedule. Bob decided to remain employed as the Director of Operations for produce packaging and he is now in a much happier place. Transitioning from the machines, he still engineers 20% of the time, but the rest of the week he is travelling or designing new products which support the output of the machines. He enjoys liaising with oversees suppliers through trips abroad and client meetings. The new role means that he travels frequently and he's often found 'talking' more often than 'engineering' which is a perfect fit for him. He has decided to put his dreams of the repair shop on hold for a few years and now puts it in his mind as a retirement option. This experiment gave him, and his employer, a fresh new approach to the way they did business and Bob proved to himself that he *can* be an entrepreneur while still being employed!

Scenario three: Bob is so enthralled with his new role that he decides to push the envelope a little further and act as a consultant for Pro-Bel. Working three days a week, he continues to enable them to design new products and ideas. The other two days a week, he visits other manufacturers and engineering firms and assists them with the creation of new revenue streams and product developments. He is now a consultant and coach on a mentorship programme and has recently delivered a talk at Reading University to MBA and engineering students who are keen to understand market segments and product life-cycles. Bob is really on a roll and he's really delighted to be helping so many people while getting paid for his advice!

Given Bob's situation, you can see that within each of the above scenarios, he has dramatically improved his life by becoming more entrepreneurial. You may be wondering if there is a way in which you too can analyse the company you work for and find a way to engage more fully with the top-level activities of the firm. Would it be possible for you to discover the challenges faced by your boss or the company directors? Could you possibly make some time to shift your focus away from the day-to-day role and develop a 'project' for yourself in the evenings and weekends? By building up a business case and researching the company, their competitors and the clients, you may very well be on your way to discovering your own entrepreneurial talents and facing the same three scenarios Bob is presented with. The window of opportunity exists for you. You just need to discover a gap which your boss may not have noticed.

This could be a tricky endeavour if you have a difficult or overpowering boss with a fragile ego. They might not take too kindly to an employee meddling in their affairs! If this is the case, either ask for permission first or leave your job and seek employment elsewhere, preferably somewhere with an open-minded management team. When you are ready to shine, embark on your quest. Any firm who wishes to grow will be only too delighted to have an entrepreneurial employee. You will soon discover, as Bob did, that the opportunities following on from such an endeavour could be numerous and endlessly rewarding. If you are remotely apprehensive about asking your employer, you might benefit from staging the entrance to your entrepreneurial experiment under the guise of training. How about asking your boss whether you can undertake a leadership or business course or if they can fund a product design, market research, marketing or start-up programme to enable you to learn *and then apply* your knowledge with them?

Most employers encourage and support training and professional development courses for their employees so would most likely be expecting this to benefit the company, so you will have the opportunity to share your research with your boss and feel less inlined to be secretive about your goals.

THE END... (OR IS IT?)

You've got to take risks if you're going to succeed.
I would much rather ask forgiveness than permission.

Sir Richard Branson

February 2022

It was a shock, at first. So many faces I recognised and so many warm hugs and warm hands accompanied by red-rimmed eyes and sadness in our hearts.

I was at Dawn's funeral. Held in the most magnificent church, a place called Gorton Monastery where she often spent her time immersed in the Spiritual – an enduring passion of hers. If she wasn't on a meditation retreat in Bali, she'd be here, as a minister. Tremendous arches and intricately carved sandstone pillars ascended up in delicate arcs of astonishing symmetry to create a spectacularly impressive vaulted ceiling. The place felt truly sacred. Positively humming with hundreds of well-wishers, it captured the energy of Dawn. The church halls were echoing with the sound of chattering and consolation, and everyone was gathered in the most incredible act of mutual sympathy. Celebrating the life of one of the *greatest* entrepreneurs that the UK has ever seen.

My eyes stung. Tears pricked at the back of my eyes as the service was read. My heart was as heavy as a stone. Only a couple of weeks had passed since her sudden death and my final and determined resignation from my own business. I was adrift once more. But this is the life of an entrepreneur. We seek freedom. Freedom above all else is why we do what we do. A Joyful Warrior knows that once they have attained it, they can quickly settle into the groove of routine and comfort and with it, the inevitable feeling of stuckness and suffocation. Once one mountain has been scaled we mustn't sit on the summit for too long. We must either seek to scale a greater part of the ridge, or descend back to the valley again, and seek the next mountain to climb. One more impressive than the last.

Author Robert Greene was interviewed for his book *Mastery* and he says:

'Calatrava was a hugely famous architect who I interviewed for this book. Calatrava would say that the greatest danger he faced when designing a building is after five, six years of working on a project it would go stale and it no longer felt alive to him and he didn't know why he was doing it. It was a terrible feeling. So, whenever that happened what he would do is reassess it, and then throw everything out. He'd throw out all of the drawings, all of the six years of work and start over. People would look at him like he was crazy but he did it because he had to get back to that 'freshness' that he needed. To be more creative and 'in the moment'. And he said, "I didn't care. I don't care if I have to throw it all out, throwing away six years of work. The feeling of making it better and being more alive in the moment is what matters.'"

Every entrepreneur will tell you unequivocally that there's simply no such thing as going backwards. The work you put out into the world has your fingerprint on it. Your ideas, designs and your brand is your personal signature. Whether it fails, scales, burns to the ground or sells is somewhat irrelevant. You will always, and forever, be known as the innovator who brought it to life. Other entrepreneurs recognise you. Those in industry who have seen your project will know your name and when an opportunity arises, they will be sure to pick up the phone and cut you in on the deal. Other entrepreneurs know the path of the Joyful Warrior. They too have failed.

Of the incredible mass of people gathered at the funeral, a good dozen I recognised. Dawn often ran events and brought a lot of us together with her never-ending enthusiasm for connecting people. One of whom was the remarkably sharp, witty and engaging chap called John Woodruffe. John had been with Dawn for most of her career and is a character who Dawn refers to as her 'maverick'. A corporate business consultant with such acute business acumen he was (according to Dawn) one of the reasons she was able to scale her business to the global brand it is today. Another close friend of Dawn's stretched her arms out and came forward for a hug. This was Nikki. A breathtaking force of nature and one of the strongest women I've ever known. Nikki Pope and I knew each other long before she and Dawn had become good friends. I rented a room in her house for several years when I was in my very early twenties. Before I had travelled to Australasia and again, when I was making my career change in my late twenties. It's just fascinating how some people are present in your life at those most pivotal moments, and then seem to reappear again when the next pivot arrives. Like a trig. point or a cairn on a perilous adventure. A warm and reassuring signal that you are journeying in parallel, that you made the key milestones and that you are somehow connected by an invisible thread. Nikki is a successful property developer and commanding swimmer who has completed and overseen six relay swims across the English Channel. It's easy to see why she and Dawn were friends. Next, was Marina Nicolas. A beautiful and charismatic international author and award winning entrepreneur. I hadn't seen Marina since my daughter was a baby and we were equally pleased to see each other and share our news; in the strange way people communicate as they mourn the loss of a shared friend. It's a strange paradox, being excited to see someone and being utterly heartbroken at the same time.

February soon transitioned to March, then March to April and my family and I were adjusting to our new way of life. We'd moved to a remote farmhouse in the wildest part of Derbyshire and I was struggling to accept the absence of my business. A huge gaping hole had been blown through the middle of my life. Both Dawn, and Rotunda. I cried for them both in equal measure. One was the child, the other was the midwife. Both gone in one sudden swoop. As the path of the warrior goes, these days are stuff of legend. The explorer in me had been searching for this. A sad but strangely empowering and validating time. Ah, I had been here before. I recognised it well. Unshackled from the grip of something which had me mercilessly bound and once again totally free to return to the creative zone which can *only* be attained with a brand-new start-up. I read back through my earlier diaries, seeking to grasp the truth of the final year or so in my business. At the very end, I concluded that I was exhausted, frustrated, stuck and (as my coach had also concluded!) bored. I think this is a common finality for the start-up creative who thrives on the buzz of innovation and enjoys the freedom to lead fully and intentionally with her heart and soul.

Marina Nicholas, John Woodruffe, Nikki Pope and three other industry heavyweights had immediately offered opportunities for me in the midst of this difficult transition. Incredibly, our connection and mutual admiration for each other's work brought forth half a dozen magnificent business collaborations. Marina and I share a passion for wellness retreats. Our complementary skills have the potential to generate the most wholesome and nourishing enterprise. We created a brand called 'Encircle' and drafted up a schedule of retreats both in the UK and abroad.

John Woodruffe also came forward. He and his team are exceptionally skilled at manufacturing, joinery and design. Over the course of six months, we designed the most beautiful contemporary brand 'Enso' which was more powerful than my previous brand and had a product design which has international potential. Nikki Pope, already a property developer, asked to see an investor proposal for my new 'Eco-Village' model, which if executed as I envision, would deliver low-cost off-grid eco-housing on a rental model, nestled in nature reserves with community gardens and craft workshops. Bringing a valuable alternative type of lifestyle to young families across the UK.

This runs in conjunction with a charity my friend and industry colleague, Annabel is building with me and a few other trustees. We've called it 'The Natural Building Foundation' which trains builders and developers in heritage building skills like thatching, straw-bale building and roundwood pole framing. This connects up with national environmental initiatives and we're actively seeking land to build a training centre and wildlife reserve. Annabel is one of the UK's handful of skilled natural builders and the most trustworthy, loyal friend one could hope to have. At the same time as negotiating all of these exciting plans with Marina, John, Nikki and Annabel, a successful and well-respected diversification entrepreneur called Robert Tate and his equally impressive wife also reached out. Robert's wife, Shelly, is about as close as you can get to Anita Roddick. At the time, she was travelling out to cocoa plantations in Colombia in order to negotiate trade deals and bring the very best ecologically sound and ethically sourced chocolate into farm shops and restaurants in the UK. We spent months drawing up plans for a potential leisure and service based business for wedding venues.

Quite simply. There are simply too many opportunities now. I can't possibly run with all of them. Amazingly, all of the new project potentials fit with my ethos, my aspirations and desires for a better, greener, more abundant natural world. All of the people I have the opportunity to partner with are established, are credible and have a proven track record in industry. Everyone I choose to work with has a really sound set of ethics. The path ahead ascends gently, levelling out to a smoother trail, branching off into dozens of exciting tracks, all of which are surrounded by rich, vibrant and colourful vistas. The sheer dramatic rock faces of my past are (mostly) behind me. I can now say that the path looks much, much more obvious and the rewards of my future businesses will be much greater than those before it. So, to conclude, I *genuinely believe* that being an entrepreneur is the best career on the planet; but those of us who choose it have chosen the most difficult path. The path of the warrior. Our joyful optimism will carry us ever onwards.

Remember me telling you that an entrepreneur works for free at the beginning. Entrepreneurs work for equity. You can't set up a business and be on a killer salary from the start. Not unless you've got an incredibly positive cash flow model or a very understanding investor. One needs to be in a sound financial position to work for free. You may not be in that position. I certainly wasn't in 2022. I suffered huge financial losses when my business was stripped bare by my remaining directors. Those who were left to safeguard the company. But this is part of the journey. I am still working on a legal case against them but it looks like it'll take many years yet to fully document, evidence and resolve.

Remember this, dear soon-to-be warrior. 'There are *innovators* and there are *imitators*'. You are the innovator. Never forget that. The vehicle will change many times but your energy and ideas will fuel them. Being an innovative entrepreneur is like being a mother. Or like being a woman. It's not about the type of business, the length of time it takes to reach success or the problems you face once you have built it, it's simply a *state of being*. As any artist will attest (building a business is a work of art), they can't just create one piece of art and sit on that for their entire life. If you are sharing your ideas with the world, share them. A great artist will have a collection of work. A musician creates a collection of albums, and an author a series of books. All crafted beautifully in the artist's own unique style and each piece an evolution of the last. The goal here is to think about your collection. The next piece in my collection of works is going to outshine anything I have created before. I know this because I am a creator. I create, practice, create again and fine-tune my work as I go. This will be the same for you too.

That being said, there are times in our journey in which we need to gather our strength. Once you've been wounded in battle, whether emotionally or physically, you need to heal.

I discovered that jumping head-first into another business start-up was not enabling me to bring my most empowered self to the deal. I was jumpy. I was distracted, I was angry and bitter and I was grieving. In a way, I realised that I was short-changing my new partners. I couldn't give myself fully and I lacked the ability to trust. They still see the Joyful Warrior, but I was injured and deeply traumatised by the betrayal. I had legal battles on my mind. Clients who still needed me. I am coming out of the darkness now but I need to train again. Rest. Build up my strength and then hit the industry with the energy and dynamism that a new enterprise deserves.

So, please remember to take a breath. Take some time. Go and get a job with a friend or associate for a while which will motivate you and give you a sense of purpose and security again. Ensure that if you do, it's in complete alignment with your mission and values. Not only does that strengthen and reaffirm your authentic voice but it might just form part of your next start-up. If you are lucky, it could be that whilst you're regaining your strength you find a new partner or investor for a collaborative project. Help someone else on their journey. Reflect. Write. Speak. Nourish your soul with creativity. Apologise to those who must wait for you if you're not ready to begin again so soon. But, begin you must. Scale the next mountain, you will. Next time, you'll be scaling it with a greater depth of vision and the wisdom of experience behind you.

On that note. Adieu, my warrior friend. This is the end. But not the end of the path.

Most importantly ... go. Start now. Start dreaming, creating, innovating.

The world needs the female entrepreneur to nurture and guide us all into a new way of doing business. You're just the woman for the job.

I believe in you. Good Luck.